SOMERSET
CURIOUS AND SURPRISING

In the Good Old Days

JACK SWEET

This book is dedicated to the memory of my late wife Margaret and remembering her great support and patience during the many years of my writing adventures.

First published in Great Britain in 2021

Copyright © Jack Sweet

All rights reserved. No part of this publication may be reproduced, stored in a retrieval system, or transmitted in any form or by any means without the prior permission of the copyright holder.

British Library Cataloguing-in-Publication Data
A CIP record for this title is available from the British Library

ISBN 978 0 85704 356 6

Halsgrove
Halsgrove House,
Ryelands Business Park,
Bagley Road, Wellington, Somerset TA21 9PZ
Tel: 01823 653777   Fax: 01823 216796
email: sales@halsgrove.com

Part of the Halsgrove group of companies
Information on all Halsgrove titles is available at: www.halsgrove.com

Printed and bound in India by Parksons Graphics Ltd

1. Introduction 4
2. Outings and Excursions 5
3. Queen Elizabeth's Coronation 1953 9
4. Club Walks. 16
5. Thrills in the Air 19
6. 'The Brighter Cary Club' 23
7. Buffalo Bill Comes to Town 26
8. The Simple Life. 29
9. The Road to Manchester 32
10. Bridgwater's Fifth of November Carnival. 40
11. Cycling in 1930 44
12. Martock's Patriotic Enthusiasm in June 1900 47
13. The *Western Gazette* Sports August 1911 50
14. The South Somerset Music Competition 52
15. 'Dinah Mite' and 'The Flamingo Club' .54
16. Kissing in Somersetshire and a Few Somerset Sayings 59
17. The End of the Second World War 63
18. Fun at the Fête 69
19. Through the Heart of Somerset. 75
20. The 'Wayzgoose' 77
21. 'Wurts, Looking at a Field of Wheat and an Old Yellow Waggon' 80
22. Yeovil Show's Centenary 87
23. The Boys' Brigade Camp – 1906 89
24. The Foresters' Fête 91
25. Clevedon's Bank Holiday and Flower Show 1910. 94
26. A 'Respectably Established' Cricket Club. 96
27. Queen Victoria's Diamond Jubilee 99
28. Blue Anchor Holiday Memories 102
29. The Saturday Morning Cinema Clubs 105
30. Taunton's 'Coronatia' Fête 108
31. The Borough Centenary 111
32. Two Victorian Wedding Celebrations 113
33. Six Days of Fun 117
34. Song and Dance in December 1972 121
35. Mistletoe, Prizes and a Sumptuous Spread 124
36. Old Christmas Time 127
37. Going a-Wassailing 131
38. A Week of Pantomimes 1951 and 'Mother Goose' 1953 133
39. New Year 1950 139
40. And Finally – Seasides in Focus 142
Sources and Acknowledgements 144

1
INTRODUCTION

THIS BOOK WAS conceived in April 2020 at the height of the coronavirus pandemic when this country was in the first national 'lock-down' and progressed during the summer months which followed. I compiled its contents as a tribute to the good times spent in Somerset before the virus struck and which without doubt, has changed our way of life, if not forever, at least for the next few years. It is fair to say that the circumstances of this pandemic have no parallel in our recorded history during the previous three or four centuries.

So please read on and sample some of the good old days enjoyed in my native county – the lovely 'Land of Summer'.

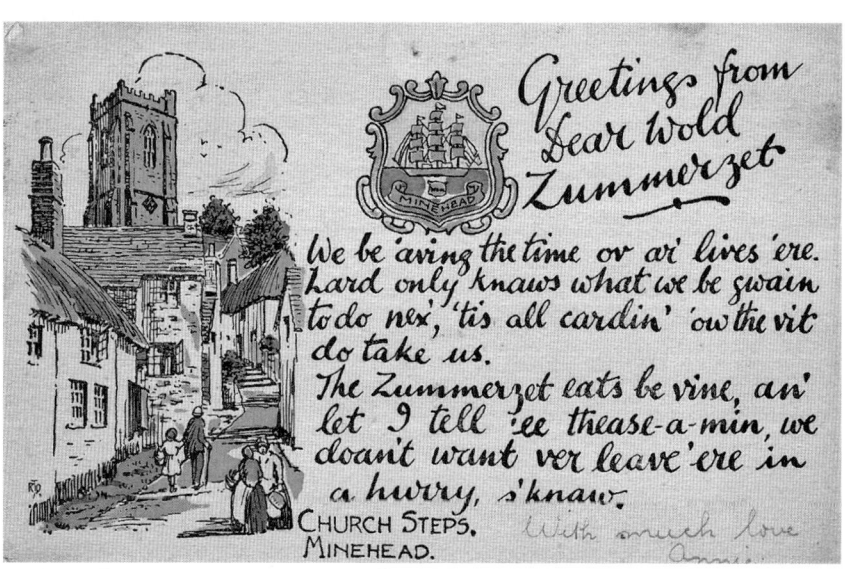

A postcard sent from Minehead in July 1940.

2

OUTINGS AND EXCURSIONS

Outings and excursions have without doubt provided some of the best of good times in many people's lives and for some, it may well have been the first time they saw the sea or another part of their county. So, let's take for example July 1925 as a typical month for summer outings and excursions from towns and villages across Somerset.

On Tuesday 8 July, some 110 'old folks' of Bridgwater aged 70 years and over were taken on their annual outing in four charabancs supplied by Mr J. Meaker of the North Street Garage to Weston Zoyland airfield to watch the Royal Air Force's 'flying operations' following which they journeyed on to Taunton. Here 'the main streets were driven through returning by the new road to Thurloxton and Huntworth' where they enjoyed a 'sumptuous tea' in the grounds of Huntworth House, the residence of the Rev. and Mrs T. T. Pryce-Mitchell. Tea was followed by 'sports and competitions for prizes' and an open-air variety show performed by the Bridgwater Merry Makers. In the words of the *Taunton Courier* on Wednesday 9 July 'A happy time was spent by all and a vote of thanks was given to the Rev. and Mrs Pryce-Mitchell for the loan of their lovely grounds. Bridgwater was reached about 9 p.m., after a memorable day.' The weather was perfect.

The Taunton Victorian Choir went on 11 July by charabanc to Minehead where they enjoyed a tea at Greensleigh Farm and travelled on to Porlock Weir to spend 'a delightful hour'. Back to Minehead for the evening and home to Taunton arriving at about half-past ten after 'a very happy outing'.

Ladies of the Taunton St James' Monday Evening and Tuesday Afternoon Mothers' Union took their annual summer's outing to West Bay where they 'all spent a thoroughly happy day', walking across the cliffs and 'sun baking' on the seafront. Tea followed at the West Bay Hotel returning home by half-past nine.

Members of the Yeovil South Street Baptist Church setting off for an outing from outside Newnam Memorial Hall on South Street in the early 1920s. Note the solid rubber tyres on the charabanc.

The *Taunton Courier* reported that on Sunday 11 July, the Great Western Railway Company's Sunday Afternoon Excursion (cost two shillings and sixpence) from Taunton Station to Watchet and Minehead had carried over 250 passengers to spend several hours at each stop in glorious sunshine. The excursion had been such a success the company planned cheap trips to Weston-super-Mare, Torquay and Paignton.

On 24 July the *Somerset Standard* reported that Frome's Angel and Crown Sick Benefit Club's annual outing had taken members to Cheddar, Axbridge, Clevedon and Portishead where 'a pleasant halt was made at each place' finishing with an evening in Bristol, all paid for by the Lamb Brewery Company.

In the same edition, the *Standard* wrote that ladies of the Holy Trinity Mothers' Union went by charabanc to Sidmouth for their annual outing leaving Frome at eight o'clock in the morning, stopping at Ilminster for lunch and reaching Sidmouth at about half-past noon. The weather was perfect and the 'party enjoyed themselves in several ways'. After tea at Trump's Hotel, Sidmouth was left at 7.30 pm and home reached some three and a half hours later at eleven o'clock.

According to the *Bath Chronicle* of 18 July, the' journeymen butchers of Bath' took their fifth annual outing to Weymouth on the previous Monday, the 13th, riding in 'four pneumatic-tyred charabancs'. In 1925 many charabancs rode on solid rubber – tyred wheels which to say the least could be hard on the passengers' bottoms. The *Chronicle* went on to record that 'The party who did not return until Tuesday had a good day with no rain. Refreshments were taken in alfresco fashion by the roadside.' The outing was supported by the Bath Butchers' Association but the *Chronicle* was silent on how the rest of the day was spent and at what time on Tuesday the party arrived back at Bath.

On Thursday 16 July, accompanied by their wives and friends the Beechen Cliff Male Voice Choir headed off at half-past one from the Old Bridge by charabanc bound for Cheddar where they visited the caves and at four o'clock took tea at the Cliff Hotel. After tea, the choir 'rendered two or three glees on the hotel lawn giving much pleasure to a large number of visitors'. On to Weston-super-Mare for an 'enjoyable two hours' before heading to Flax Bourton and the home of Mr and Mrs White where the choir sang and took some refreshment before arriving home at about eleven o'clock. The *Bath Chronicle's* report of the outing revealed that the charabancs had been supplied by the Bath Electric Tramway Co Ltd.

From Street on Saturday morning 11 July at eleven o'clock, a party from the Wesleyan Sunday School and Bible classes left on a special train bound for the delights of Burnham-on-Sea, arriving just after mid-day. They quickly assembled on the sands for games of rounders, tennis, cricket and 'other delights of the seaside'. Tea was taken at Mrs Marchant's Tea Gardens where '170 people did simple justice to all the good things provided'. The party arrived back tired but happy at Street just after nine o'clock and in the words of the *Central Somerset Gazette,* 'the outing was an outstanding success'.

On Wednesday 15 July, youngster and their teachers of the Meare Congregational Sunday School also travelled to Burnham-on-Sea for their annual outing. Most left by train from Glastonbury Station, but a few 'were taken by Mr Phelp's lorry'. The weather was fine, there was 'a very nice tide' and tea was taken at Mrs Marchant's Tea Gardens. Arriving back at Glastonbury later that evening tired but happy, the youngsters were met by 'Messrs H. Ford, Bert Baker and J. Phelps who conveyed the tired party home from the Station'.

Some 80 scholars, teachers and parents of the Stoke St Michael Wesleyan Sunday School left the village at 8 o'clock on the morning of 6 July and travelled by charabanc to Weston-super-Mare via Cheddar Gorge reaching the seaside just after ten. Here they split up, some to play on the sands, whilst others visited the 'old Pier, or went shopping. At half-past four the children gathered for tea at Brown's Café, following which everyone once again went their separate ways to re-assemble at eight o'clock to travel home via Burrington Combe at about ten after in the words of the *Wells Journal* 'a most delightful day'.

The various outings are but a snapshot of the many enjoyed by Somerset folk of all ages during that summer of 1925.

3

QUEEN ELIZABETH'S CORONATION 1953

IT COULD BE said that in 1953 that the nation finally put the hardships and shortages of the war years behind us when on 4 February sweet rationing ended, three weeks later wartime deserters from the armed forces were granted amnesty and on 29 May, Edmund Hillary and Sherpa Tenzing stood on the summit of Mount Everest. 1953 would also be Coronation year and the start of a new 'Elizabethan Age' when everyone could enjoy themselves and look forward to a better and brighter future.

The Coronation of Queen Elizabeth II was held on Tuesday 2 June and on 29 May the *Western Gazette* announced that:

'The flags are up, bonfires are being prepared, the souvenir gifts are ready for distribution, the food and drink have been ordered – and the south and west is all set to celebrate the Coronation. If the sun shines on Tuesday, town and countryside will be in the gayest mood within memory. The Coronation will bring a resurgence of much that is best in the English tradition, particularly the Elizabethan, for plays, pageants, maypole dancing and characteristic rural revelries will again grace the village green and recreation ground. As darkness falls at the end of a memorial day, the countryside will be starred by the beacon lights of innumerable bonfires on the great eminencies which through the centuries have flashed their signals on historic occasions.'

For weeks Yeovil people planned for the big day, there would be street parties, dancing, sports, fancy dress parades, concerts, fireworks and bonfires, plus all manner of jollification for young and old alike. Television first came to the Southwest late in 1952 and sets were still comparatively scarce, people were planning TV parties to watch the Coronation 'live' from London (in black and white).

The Yeovil and District Chamber of Trade organised 'Yeovil Shopping Week' from 22 to 30 May as their contribution to the town's celebrations and to show 'the public the advantages and great facilities offered by this ancient market town with its wide range of shops catering for every need'. The 'Week' included competitions for the best-decorated buildings and window displays. Radio House in Princes Street won the best-decorated premises in the 25 feet and under category, and Vincent's Motor Works were the winners of the 25 feet and above class.

Coronation week was the school half-term break and several held Coronation parties on the Friday when everyone broke up for the holidays. There was some drama at the Huish Infants School party when five-years-old Sandra Jones, of Westland Road, ate the small round object which fell out of the cracker she had just pulled, thinking it was a sweet. It was, in fact, an indoor firework, and Sandra was rushed to hospital where she was treated and then sent home.

On Sunday evening, 31 May, there was a 'Grand Coronation Concert' in Sidney Gardens given by the Yeovil Workmen's Silver Prize Band, resplendent in their new dark blue and red uniforms, and The Yeovil Girls Choir who were appearing in their new emerald green frocks made by Mrs H.A. Martin. The Concert, compered by Mr W.R. Consitt, began at 7.25 pm when the Band sounded a Special Coronation Fanfare.

Over fifty Yeovil Girl Guides spent nearly four hours on 28 May cleaning the War Memorial in The Borough and on the next Sunday, following the Civic Coronation Service, a wreath was laid at the memorial in memory of the town's fallen in the two World Wars.

As usual with our national celebrations, Coronation Day dawned overcast and grey, there were showers and sunny intervals and it was not too warm. However, come what may the day was going to one to be remembered.

St John's church bells rang out in the early morning and the *Western Gazette* reported that: 'Yeovil wore a brilliant and defiant cloak of gaiety on Tuesday in spite of the chilly showers and wind which threatened to spoil the town's celebration – which were concentrated mainly on the entertainment of the children. The only effect the weather had was to create a certain amount of confusion in areas where a large number of parties was being held, with the result that everyone made for the same shelter and four or five different streets made for the same shelter and four or five different streets attempted to hold their parties in the same place, however, difficulty was overcome by the organisers giving up the task of trying to discriminate between the separate parties.'

The Mayor and Mayoress, Councillor and Mrs William Austin, made a six-hour tour of the town's street parties, starting at Cecil Street, and in the evening, the mayor lit the first firework at the Coronation firework display on Summerhouse Hill. The Yeovil Scouts lit the bonfire on the top of the hill and a bonfire beacon at the Hundred Stone, Mudford Road. The mayor was also honoured by the award by the Queen of the Coronation Medal.

The five babies born in the town on Coronation Day were presented with special souvenirs by the Borough Council.

Coronation evening saw a folk and square-dancing display in Sidney Gardens given by The Yeovil Branch of the English Folk Song and Dance Society, followed by general dancing to music from an amplified radiogram.

The Record Sales Chart was just seven months old in June 1953 and naturally reflected the Coronation theme. Chart-toppers that month included *In a Golden Coach* sung by 'heart-throb' Dickie Valentine, Billy Cotton and His Band were also at the top with the same number alongside Winifred Atwell beating out the *Coronation Rag* on her piano.

Street parties had been a feature of the VE and VJ celebration at the end of the War in 1945 and were revived again in 1953 for the Coronation of Queen Elizabeth II. All across Yeovil people had established committees and groups to organise street parties, food and drink was bought, housewives made cakes and prepared sandwiches, TV sets were set up in houses and halls for communal viewing of the Coronation, entertainment organised along with the hundred and one things to make the day a memorable one.

Nearly every street in Yeovil would have a party, some organised by the street itself, some streets grouped together to provide one big party. By far the greatest number of parties were held on Coronation Day but some were held in the days which followed.

The mayor and mayoress, toured the Coronation Day parties, beginning in Cecil Street where they were presented with a bouquet by Julie Sullivan. The Cecil Street party incorporated Reckleford, Court Ash, Mary Street,

Market Street and lower Silver Street. There was a fancy dress competition, old age pensioner's quiz, a ladies ankle competition, a knobbly knees contest, a Punch and Judy Show given by Mr D. Silver, and Mr Wilburn's ventriloquist act. Tea followed the entertainment and there was dancing in Cecil Street.

The Chilton Grove party included a TV show in a marquee and there were pony rides.

At Larkhill there was a 'comic football match between men and women' and the day ended with dancing on the wide grass verge at the side of Larkhill Road.

A fancy dress procession of 100 children, led by decorated wagons and the Mayfair Dance Orchestra, opened the Coronation Avenue area celebrations and proceeded to St Peter's Church Hall where the fancy dress judging took place. There were sideshows, amusements and a comic football match followed by a programme of sports, including a darts contest. Over 200 children each received a souvenir mug filled with sweets and an ice cream. The evening concluded with a cabaret show presented by St Peter's Youth Club.

Mr Mike Loveless cuts the cake at the Orchard Street Coronation Party in the Yeovil Huish Baptist Chapel Sunday Schoolroom.

Westland Sports Club and ground was chosen by the Seaton Road area for their celebration and over 120 youngsters had tea, sports and a fancy dress competition. The sports club was shared with Westbourne Grove whose 93 children sat down to tea opposite the Seaton Road contingent.

The aim of the Orchard Street committee was for everyone in the street to celebrate, so the children's tea party was held in the Huish Baptist Sunday Schoolroom in the afternoon and followed by a tea for the adults. Mr Mike

Loveless gave both parties and he can be seen in the photograph cutting the Coronation cake at the children's party. Later, there was a general social evening with games and a community singsong.

Queen Street lived up to its name with a triumphal arch entwined with ever-greens and festooned with bunting and patriotic emblems at the entrance to the street.

Nearly a dozen children in Chelston Avenue who were ill in bed had their tea brought to them by Mr F. M. Quinton, dressed as a clown, who also left a 1 lb. tin of biscuits at the houses of old folk and widows.

There was a roundabout for the children of Milford Road and prizes were awarded for the best-decorated houses.

A feature of the St George's Avenue party was a film show in Milford Infants School watched by over 140 youngsters who each received a souvenir book, an orange and sweets. The grown-ups enjoyed an evening of dancing in the school hall and a buffet.

In Milford Junior School, the Upper Chelston Avenue and St David's Crescent party was led by a barrel organ. There was tea for 130 children with souvenir mugs for the under fives and savings certificates for the under 15s.

The St Michael's Avenue and Sherborne Road area held their party in Pen Mill School where there was a TV show followed by an afternoon of sports, a fancy dress parade, games, then tea, followed by more sports and finally dancing and community singing in the playground.

The fancy dress procession which opened the Lyde Road party was led by the Salvation Army Young People's Band and a telegram was sent to the Queen from the children.

At Hillside Terrace, off Sherborne Road, the party was concluded with a grandstand view of the fireworks and bonfire on Summerhouse Hill after an enjoyable tea, Punch and Judy Show, and a comic football match.

At Summerleaze Park, over 3000 hand-made flowers were included in window and porch boxes and something like 2000 feet of bunting made up the band of red, white and blue which encircled the road; thirty banners on 12-foot poles were placed around the cul-de-sac.

The main attraction of the Summerlands street party was a baby show won by Ian Rees in the under 12 months class and John Feaver was first in the one to two years old class.

Maypole dancing was included in the Preston Road programme together with a film show and a whist drive.

There were so many parties and events that I have only been able to give a very brief description but perhaps the *Western Gazette's* report on celebrations in Westland Road gives a flavour of the day:

'In a marquee erected at the foot of the decorated cul-de-sac, Nos. 117 to 149 Westland Road, Yeovil, the residents and their children, a company of 100, held a Coronation Day street party. Mr and Mrs S. Gibbs (No135) were the organisers and Mr Gibbs also provided a television set. The 36 children were given tea and they also enjoyed the large Coronation cake given by Mr Gibbs. Games for all followed and buffet refreshments were provided, with wines and beer in the evening to drink the health of the Queen.

'Mr Brian Gibbs played the piano and Mr K. Edward the drums for community singing and dancing in the marquee and the street until midnight. Each boy received a Coronation mug and pencil and each girl a mug and handkerchief as well as oranges. At the close, the thanks of the residents were expressed by Mr Russell to the organisers. The cost of the party was met by house to house collections.'

On Saturday 6 June the Coronation Festival of Youth was held at the Huish football ground and the following week's *Western Gazette* reported that

'Many of the pre-service uniformed organisations (there was compulsory military National Service at the time) and youth groups in the district had combined to present the Coronation Festival of Youth at the football ground.

'The three-and-a-half-hours programme commenced with a procession from the Town Station headed by a combined band of the Air Training Corps, the Girls' Training Corps and Scouts. The local Boys' Brigade band brought up the rear.

'After the assembly, the Parade Marshal Lieut. A Barker (officer commanding Yeovil unit Sea Cadet Corps), accompanied by the mayor and mayoress went on a tour of inspection and this was followed by the naval routine of hoisting the colours and a march past.

'The first display was of the Holgar Neilson artificial respiration, a new method which had recently been introduced into this country from

Denmark, given by members of the British Red Cross Society Cadet Unit 2677. A commentary on the proceedings was given by Commandant D. McVeigh (VAD Somerset/19 BRC).

'Seven members of the St Peter's Boys' Club were matched against seven from the 1st Yeovil company, The Boys' Brigade, at cycle football but after many laughs, thrills and spills in this novel event the score sheets remained blank. Those taking part were: – St Peter's – Michael Grinter, John Creek, Keith Burgess, Derek Rendall, David Monhurel, John Fisk and Arthur Johns; The Boys' Brigade – Joe Arnold, Bruce Trigger, Trevor Broomhall, Alwyn Powell, Anthony Hazell, Alan Montacute and Peter Norris.

'Exercises on the mat, parallel bars and vaulting horse were given by the St John's Gymnasium and Athletic Club's display team under Gym Leader G. Loveless, and members of the local Guide companies entertained by creating flags, culminating in the Union Jack from rolls of red, white and blue material.

'Further displays were given by the Yeovil Girls' Training Corps (PT to music) and members of the Girls Life Brigade (folk and square dancing) and a model camp pitched by local Scouts caused much interest.'

The *Western Gazette* went on to write that:

'Two of the four young people chosen to represent Somerset at the Commonwealth Youth Service at Westminster Abbey, on Sunday, were from Yeovil. They were Keith Clark and Brenda Clark (no relation) – both of St Peter's (Westfield) Youth Club. Although the Yeovil unit, Sea Cadet Corps (Grass Royal) has only been in operation for about three months, one of its members was chosen to represent the Corps at the Coronation ceremony in London. He was Michael Barrett, son of Mr and Mrs R. J. Barrett of 104 Sherborne Road, Yeovil. Michael's position was at the Queen Victoria Memorial outside Buckingham Palace. Among the contingent of the Boys' Brigade to attend the Coronation were three members of local companies: – Sergt. T. Montacute, 1st Yeovil; Sergt. R. Creek, 1st Stoke; Sergt. A. Hawker, 2nd Dorchester. The BB contingent of 600 members had places outside Buckingham Palace.'

4

CLUB WALKS

ONE OF THE highlights of the village year during the latter years of the 19th century and into the early years of the 20th was the Annual Feast or Walking Day of members of the village Friendly Society. Friendly Societies grew up during the late 18th and 19th centuries when groups of people joined together and contributed small sums of money for distribution to members in times of sickness, old age and to cover funeral expenses to avoid being 'buried on the parish'. Some societies grew into national organisations, such as the Oddfellows and the Foresters, but in those days the majority were local and found in small towns and villages.

Many of these local societies or 'Clubs', as they were commonly called, would select a summer day for a celebration, the members would dress in their Sunday Best, parade around the village often behind their symbols or emblems, and generally have a good time with feasts and other 'jollifications'. It must be remembered that in those not so far off times, day to day life could be pretty hard, and the occasional celebrations or treats were something to look forward to and enjoy.

However, with the introduction of universal pensions and benefits, apart from some of the national friendly societies, few local 'Clubs' have continued into the early decades of the 21st century (at least not in their original form).

The *Western Gazette's* reports of the 'Club' days make interesting reading and provide a valuable reminder of those times when local people 'clubbed' together to ensure some small financial security in misfortune and a decent burial.

On Monday 10 July 1899, sixty-eight members of the West Coker Friendly Society, dressed in their Sunday best, met at the village school, and led by the Crewkerne 'Star of the West' band, visited the Rectory, and then marched to the parish church for a service, following which the

The Haselbury Club.

procession reformed and visited the residences of prominent members of the village community. The highlight of the day was the Club dinner held in a marquee in one of Mr Cave's fields, with the 'excellent spread provided by Mr Guy of the New Inn'. During the evening there were 'the usual attractions in the field and cinematograph views were shown in a tent'.

The 1906 annual festival of the Montacute Provident and Mutual Benefit Society was held on Monday 18 June, and 'the weather being all that could be desired'. promptly at 9 o'clock on that sunny June morning, some 70 members assembled outside the parish church, and after answering their names went inside for the 'special service'. Filing outside at the end of the service, the members formed up behind the Kingsbury Brass Band, and with the Society's banner leading the way processed around the village calling at the houses of their supporters and patrons. Dinner was served in the National School by Mr Guppy of the Phelips Arms and afterwards they were entertained to tea at the Vicarage. Swings were set up in the Borough and were 'well patronised'.

Haselbury Plucknett's Male and Female Friendly Societies Club Walk and Dinner took place in 'beautiful weather' on Tuesday 2 June 1908. The 100 or so 'male and female members' assembled outside the schoolroom and processed around the village behind the South Petherton Town Band. Returning to the parish church for the service conducted by the Vicar, the Reverend S. W. E. Gilliat, with the sermon preached by the Reverend G. Beilby, from Bristol, a former Haselbury vicar. Following the service, the church bells were rung and the members repaired to the Jubilee Dining Hall for the annual dinner served by Mr E. Edmunds of the Market Square, Crewkerne. After dinner, the procession reformed and marched to Manor Farm where tea was served and 'Dancing was indulged in the evening and the usual attractions were in evidence.'

The first week of June 1908, seems to have been popular with the local village Clubs because on Thursday the 4th, the Misterton Male and Female Friendly Societies held their annual festival and on the following day the Seavington St Michael Club held theirs.' The sun shone on both days, the members processed, ate their fill and no doubt enjoyed 'the usual attractions'.

5
THRILLS IN THE AIR

A Parachute Drop
A novelty which thrilled Yeovilians on Sunday 7 February 1926 was a parachute drop and which was graphically reported in the *Western Gazette*:

'Yeovil people in crowds witnessed a parachute descent on the Westland Aerodrome on Sunday afternoon. The descent was made from a height of 600 feet by Captain A.F. Muir, of the Surrey Flying Services. Coming from an "Avro" aeroplane, piloted by Flying Officer E.F. Smith, he dropped 200 feet before the parachute, a "Guardian Angel," opened out. The remaining 400 feet he came down with every appearance of ease, waving his hand cheerily to the spectators and landing in full view in front of them. It was a perfectly judged feat, and had the added interest that Captain Muir was performing it for the first time. Although it is demonstrated at most of the towns visited by Surrey Services, it is usually performed by Mr A.A. Anderson, who last year made as many as six descents in one week. In a demonstration of trick flying immediately after Captain Muir's descent, Mr Anderson and Mr B. Powell walked to the tips of the planes while the machine was circling in mid-air. The machines were very largely patronised for pleasure trips throughout their visit, and towards the end of Sunday afternoon had to refuse bookings. They left on Tuesday.'

The British Hospitals' Air Pageant
Seven years later, the British Hospitals' Air Pageant was described by the *Western Gazette* as 'the most brilliant aviation display which has yet come to Yeovil' when it was held on the Westland Airfield on Wednesday, the 7th June 1933.

The pageant was led by Mr Charles Scott, AFC, famous for record-breaking solo flights between London and Australia, and a 'galaxy of 15 "star" pilots'.

Seven machines, including the 'latest airliner, the DH Dragon,' flew over the town from the west to circle around Sherborne before heading back to the Westland Airfield. The displays which followed included one given by Mr E. W. Bond who 'flying in a Gypsy Moth equipped with a wireless made the aircraft perform in strict keeping with the rhythm of dance records, rising, diving and stalling'. Mr Bond also gave an exhibition of 'crazy flying showing with uncanny skill the things the pilot should not do in the air'.

Mr Harry Willis gave an exciting display of wing walking and Captain B. Phillips, DFC, dropped paper streamers from his Red Sparrow sports plane and then swooped down cutting the streamers before they reached the ground.

Passengers were taken up for rides in a variety of aircraft, including the DH Dragon and some braver souls flew with Captain Phillips and Flt. Lieut. Pugh, when they performed 'their daring aerobatics'. However, those who went up with Captain Phillips had the comforting knowledge that he claimed to hold the world record in carrying 66,000 passengers, chiefly in aerobatic flying, without a single injury. Flt. Lieut. Pugh claimed no such record!

A Fairey Fox thrilled the crowd with its top speed of 200 mph in comparison with the little BAC Drone built originally as a glider but now powered by a 6 hp Douglas motorcycle engine giving a top speed of 50 mph, a landing speed of 22 mph and a 60 miles range on a gallon tank of petrol.

The pageant, however, was not entirely free of incident as the *Western Gazette* reported ;

'A parachute landing made late in the evening by Mr Evans, one of the cleverest parachutists in the country, had a sensational ending. Allowing for his being carried to the aerodrome by a ten mile an hour wind, Mr Evans dropped from a height of 1,500 feet immediately over the big hangar at the western end, delayed until he had fallen 300 to 400 feet, and then opened his parachute. The wind proved much less than had been calculated, and he fell on the roof of the hangar, happily slipping clear of the glass and landing on his feet in the gutter between the two spans of the roof. He was entirely unhurt and proved an agile climber, but did not succeed in getting down from the roof for half or three-quarters of an hour.'

Westland's aerodrome in 1926.

The pageant left Westlands the following morning for the next two shows at Teignmouth and Tiverton.

RNAS Yeovilton's Naval Air Day 1947

The first post-war air day at RNAS Yeovilton was held on Saturday 7 September 1947, when HMS *Heron* entertained over 12,000 spectators to a seven hours show. The *Western Gazette* wrote that:

'The present-day task of *Heron* is the training of young naval recruits in the maintenance of all the various types of aircraft used by Naval Air Command, and it was obvious from Saturday's comprehensive programme that a lot of care had been taken to fully represent this important task to the general public. About a dozen large hangars were turned into display centres for the material and equipment used in the technical instruction of the 800 recruits at present under training.

'Visitors – who came from Yeovil, where there were long queues at Station Road for the specially augmented 'bus service – Taunton, Weymouth, Bournemouth, Shepton Mallet and other districts found a seven hours' programme organised for them and for the young children there was a playground.'

Westland Aircraft's Chief Test Pilot, Mr Harald Penrose, gave a display of 'crazy flying' in his Widgeon light aircraft and Mr Alan Bristow, flying a specially modified Westland S.51 helicopter, demonstrated the rescue of a casualty from a rubber raft floating in a water tank. Alan Bristow would one day found Bristow Helicopters.

A prototype Westland Wyvern, a large single-engine attack fighter, flew past with Squadron Leader Peter Garner at the controls, but tragically just over one month later on 15 October, he would be killed when Wyvern TS371 suffered engine failure and crashed during a test flight.

'The grand old lady of naval aviation', the Swordfish, flown by Lieut.-Commander Somerville, was followed in complete contrast by two jet aircraft, a Meteor and the Navy's new Vampire, demonstrating their speed and manoeuvrability. The flying programme included a demonstration of formation flying by the station's training squadron which ended in a lucky escape for the Flight C O, Lieut.-Commander Illingworth. On landing, his aircraft's brakes and flaps failed and the Lieut.-Commander just managed to clear the end of the aerodrome and was directed to Boscombe Down where he made a safe landing on the longer runway.

The 1947 public air show provided the Royal Navy with an excellent demonstration of its aviation capability in the emerging post-war world.

6

'THE BRIGHTER CARY CLUB'

A 'TONGUE IN CHEEK' article from the *Somerset Year Book*, published by the Society of Somerset Folk in 1926.

'There is a little mystery and some little humour behind the following extracts, which appeared in two consecutive issues in June of the *Western Gazette*. Apart from this they explain themselves.

I
'A BRIGHTER CARY CLUB,'
A CAMPAIGN OF SMILES,
(*contributed*)

'The first monthly meeting of the "Brighter Cary Club" was held on Friday to discuss several important matters, the attendance at the George Hotel being extremely good in view of the weather conditions.

'The President, the "Marquis of Barrow," in opening the meeting said he felt it a great honour to preside over such a select assembly. Their Club had been formed with the praiseworthy object of enlivening the district of Castle Cary and he was sure they were all anxious to do anything in their power to further that object. There was undoubtedly abundant scope for the activities of the Club, and he hoped they would justify their title to the full. As a beginning they had organised a most successful dance at the George Hotel, which had resulted in a substantial sum being credited to the Club funds. In concluding, the President said that he had one request to make, which was that all members of the Club should refrain from alcoholic refreshment and also from working in pairs.

'The first item to be debated was "Should Cats have Tails?" In discussing this question members pointed out that people might stroke an angry cat by mistake if it had no tail to indicate its feelings, and it was also a useful appendage as a handle to eject it before retiring for the night.

'Should Courting Couples be Permitted?' The Committee decided that this was a question over which they had no jurisdiction, but questions on the matter should be asked in Parliament.

'Should Pins have Points?' This provoked a somewhat heated discussion. The lady members maintained that pins were useless as weapons of attack unless they had points. The male members asserted that points conduced to profanity and the general lowering of the moral standard. The ladies replied that pointed pins contributed largely to material uplift in the lower portions of society.

'"Kissing is a Desirable Practice." Contrary to expectation, this subject provoked little opposition. The Secretary, however, vehemently denounced it as a weak habit, generally accelerating the promotion of disease and savouring of cheap sentiment. He was loudly hissed.

'The effect of the "Brighter Cary Club" campaign was then discussed. Members reported that they had noticed broad smiles on the faces of townspeople, which could be traced to the date of the foundation of the Club. A record amount of spring cleaning had been carried, and even the oldest inhabitants began to look young again.

'In conclusion the Chairman thanked those present for their attendance, and proposed a hearty vote of thanks to the "Marquis of Barrow" for facing a long journey in order to be with them that night. He was sure they were all grateful to him for coming. The applause was so great that the lights were extinguished, and in the interval before they were re-lit strange gurgling sounds were heard among the gathering. The meeting then dispersed in a semi-orderly manner.

II

"THE BRIGHTER CARY CLUB"

'It has been brought to our notice on behalf of "The Brighter Cary Club" that no meeting of the description given in last week's *Western Gazette* has been held, and therefore this report was imaginary.

'The contribution was forwarded to us and printed in good faith. We would suggest that the author should make his peace with the Committee of the Club, who inform us that the effects of his contribution may be that an erroneous view of the activities of the Club will be given. Mr W.

The 'Brighter Cary Club' met in the George Hotel.

Payne of the George Hotel, also protests that there has been no meeting in connection with the Brighter Cary Club as published in our issue of June 11th.

'We can only add that we hope the publicity thus given to the affair will have the effect of genuinely assisting in the attainment of the Promoters' objects.

'The following, which we have received from a far-off correspondent, has no reference to the foregoing, but seems to have been written by one who is familiar with another of the town's hostelries:

> *Britannia* needs no bulwarks,
> No steadiments beside her,
> Her strength is drawn from Cary wood,
> Containing Cadbury cider.'

7

BUFFALO BILL COMES TO TOWN

Early in July 1903, posters began appearing all over Yeovil – 'Buffalo Bill's Wild West Show' was coming to town. There would be genuine Indians, real cowboys and cowgirls, US Cavalry, English Lancers, Russian Cossacks, Rough Riders, Mexican Ruralies, crack shots, exciting battles and episodes from the Wild West! The Wild West Show and Congress of Rough Riders of the World personally led by Colonel W. F. Cody, 'Buffalo Bill' the 'One Grand Ruler of the Amusement World,' would thrill young and old alike for one day only on Saturday 24 July in the Agricultural Show Ground at Seaton Road.

Early on Saturday morning, four special trains drew into Hendford Goods Station and disembarked four hundred horses and seven hundred people of all nationalities watched by a large and enthusiastic crowd lining the route to the Show Ground. With military precision, the great arena measuring 325 feet by 500 feet was laid out with covered seating for nearly 15,000 spectators, and at 11 o'clock the Famous Cowboy Military Band began the day's events with the Preliminary Open Air Concert.

Guess what – it poured with rain off and on all day – but this did not dampen the spirits of the huge audiences for the two shows who kept dry under the large waterproof awnings. They came from town and country, in special trains, on foot, bicycles, carriages, wagons and in the rare motor car. By the end of the day, over 25,000 people had seen the Show and 'It was no exaggeration to say that the town had never been so full of people before,' exclaimed the *Western Gazette*.

Both performances were opened with the overture 'Star Spangled Banner' played by the Cowboy Band, followed by the 'Grand Review of the Rough Riders of the World' led in person by Buffalo Bill. Group after group of riders galloped into the arena, there were famous Indian tribes of the Western Plains – the Brule, Ogallalla, Uncappapa, Sioux, Cheyenne and

Arapahoes – followed by Mexicans, Cossacks, Arab Horsemen, Cowboys, Rough Riders, English Lancers, the Sixth and Tenth US Cavalry and Western Girls. Now followed exhibitions of riding and a display of cannon firing by US Artillerymen. A train of covered wagons drew into the arena and into a circle as it was attacked by Indians. However, after a gallant defence by cowboys and wagoners, the attackers were driven off. Indians then pursued a Pony Express rider who outrode them and safely delivered his precious mail. The Deadwood stagecoach, mud spraying from its wheels, drove wildly into the arena followed by a band of whooping Indians. Skidding to a halt, the passengers blazed away at their attackers with rifles and revolvers until Buffalo Bill and his band of cowboys came charging to the rescue in true Wild West style. There was 'an incident of ranch life in the West' when a cabin was attacked by a band of Indians on the warpath and once again the cowboys arrived in the nick of time to save the settler and his family.

Posters advertising Wild West Show appeared across Yeovil.

Buffalo Bill gave an exhibition of rifle shooting on horseback smashing glass balls thrown into the air as he galloped past. Cossacks came in at full gallop, some standing on their heads on their horses backs, other hanging under their flying steeds. Two Western American Girls raced each other, cowboys galloped around at full speed picking up handkerchiefs, lassoing horses and riding bucking bronchos. The 'Celebrated American Marksman' Johnnie Baker, standing on his head and from other strange positions, shot up targets in all parts of the arena.

The *Western Gazette* reported on re-enactments from the battle of San Juan Hill in the recently fought Spanish-American War in Cuba:

'Men who had actually taken part in the fight engaged in a couple of elaborate spectacles, the first depicting the time before the battle, and the second the storming of the hill. Detachments from Roosevelt's Rough Riders, Twenty-fourth Infantry, Ninth and Tenth Cavalry, Grime's Battery, Garcia's Cuban Scouts, Pack Train etc. etc. were introduced. Tents were pitched, campfires lighted for the bivouac and the soldiers having shown some of the sports in camp, tenderly sang "The dear little Shamrock." The contrast came with the bugle call to arms, volley firing and independent shooting and the use of a machine gun, the hill being successfully "stormed" by the infantry.'

Continuing with the military theme, English Cavalrymen who had seen active service in the Boer War in South Africa, and detachments of the 10th US Coloured Cavalry and veterans of the 6th US Cavalry, paraded the arena and demonstrated their skills.

Each performance concluded with a grand finale of the entire cast galloping around the arena to the thunderous cheers and applause of the audience.

A variety of sideshows were presented in a large tent outside the arena including Hassam Ali, the 8ft 2ins giant; Walters, the Blue man; Shanghai Chinese Troops of gymnasts, acrobats, conjurers, and the only little-footed Chinese ladies ever seen in Great Britain; Giovanni's performing cockatoos; Griffin, necromancer and sword swallower; Herr Rhoatig, wonderful manipulator of cigars etc.; Mlles Octavia, fearless serpent enchantress; Alfonso, human ostrich; and Professor Sackette's Military Band.

The *Western Gazette* wrote that: 'Through the thoughtfulness of the Mayor the lamps in the vicinity of West Hendford were allowed to remain lighted for a longer period than usual for the convenience of the people and the show employees.'

So ended an exciting day in Yeovil in the summer of 1903 but there was a postscript to these events forty-six years later in the *Western Gazette* of 4 March 1949:

> 'Former Member of Buffalo Bill Show
>
> A native of South Petherton who emigrated to Canada and went on tour for many years as a member of the famous Buffalo Bill Wild West Show, Mr Joseph Reyland, died on Saturday at the home of his daughter and son-in-law, Mr and Mrs S. Tucker, at 3 Fielding Road, where he had lived for 15 years. A veteran of the Boer War, Mr Reyland enlisted in the Canadian voluntary force at the outbreak. While in England Mr Reyland was a farm worker at Ash and Lambrook but latterly was employed by the Bristol *Evening Post* in Yeovil as a newsvendor. He was 76.'

8
THE SIMPLE LIFE

THE FOLLOWING TALE appeared in my book *Somerset Tales Shocking and Surprising* published in 2011 and as the main character was having a very good time I thought it worthy of retelling.

Dr Charles A. Fox was a retired medical practitioner and member of the Royal College of Surgeons. He came from an old West Country family, and at 64 years of age was the founder member and practitioner of 'The Simple Life' and 'Health Culture' at his home in The Birdcage', South Petherton. According to a set of four pictorial cards featuring Dr Fox, and a lady (presumably his wife), he explained at great length that both these Movements 'now interesting so many of both Sexes, tend to a return to the more natural conditions'. The cards announced that the doctor was the author of a large number of tracts and books on a wide range of subjects, including *The Interpretation of the Great Pyramid and Fairy Tales, Royal Family, Disasters, Smallpox, Epidemics, Baptism, The Salvation Army, Hiawatha, Anglo-Israelism,* and *Canaan,* to name but a few.

On 11 May 1913, *The New York Times,* wrote an account from a Special Correspondent in Taunton published by the *Daily Mirror,* on a day spent in the company of Dr Charles Fox at his South Petherton home:

'Dr Fox, who is a member of the Royal College of Surgeons, is no mere theorist. In the secluded fields and orchards round his cottage he puts his ideas into practice. Jumping and skipping and frisking like a high-spirited schoolboy. This for instance, is a typical day in his simple life:

'Rises soon after dawn; pole twirling exercises; dew bath, or ordinary bath in pool; vegetarian breakfast about 7 o'clock; running, cycling, reading, and writing during the morning; plain vegetarian meal about midday; more pole twirling in the afternoon; running and other exercises during the remainder of the day.

Dr Charles Fox enjoying the 'Simple Life' in his garden at South Petherton.

'To meet Dr Fox for the first time,' says the correspondent, 'is a surprising experience. His sudden appearance when he left his cottage to receive me was startling. It was a lovely Spring morning, and only the singing of the birds could be heard. Suddenly a soft and jaunty step sounded behind me. A twirling pole narrowly missed my head. Then I turned and saw the strangest figure of a man to be found on any country road.

'Dr Fox was dressed in the costume that he generally wears. His body was draped with a white cotton wrapper, leaving the arms bare. A pair of white calico knickers and brown stockings covered his legs, and on his feet were sandals. Long, gray-brown curls reached to his shoulders, and his hat was a curious round piece of brown felt.

'"It is very good of you to come and see me," he cried. "I am just going to have my exercise and bath in the orchard! Come with me."

'He started skipping off down the road gaily twirling a pail over his head. Under the blossoming trees, Dr Fox went through the weirdest evolutions. He ran to and fro, hopped, jumped, skipped and flung his arms about in graceful circles.

'"Grace!" he said, during a pause. "That is what Englishmen lack to-day. It is a quality which seems to have died out in modern civilization. Grace and beauty are almost lost to-day owing to our frightful rectangular form of dress."

'He continued talking rapidly. "We want to see people as they really are – the human form is full of beauty – yet men and women make their figures un-natural and hideous by their clothes. Why do men wear coats which make their shoulders square? Did Nature ever intend that man should make himself look so awful? The true and only existence is the simple life of the savage."

'Dr Fox then took his morning dew bath. The thick grass was drenched in dew, and this most ardent simple-life apostle revelled in the moisture.

'"In the summer I bathe in a pool here five times a day," he said. "I never feel the cold. All the year round I dress like this."

'After Dr Fox had dressed he walked briskly about the orchard, explaining his views. One of his favourite exercises – one which he frequently performs every day – is that of pole-twirling – twisting a light pole with the fingers above his head. "It is a splendid method," he says, "for keeping in good health."'

9

THE ROAD TO MANCHESTER

In the winter of 1949, Yeovil Town Football Club embarked on a journey which would become part of football legend and leave an indelible print on the history of the home town.

The Yeovil streets were deserted when the bells of St John's rang in 1949 and in The Borough only two young men welcomed in the New Year. However, the relative peace of the New Year was the calm before the town went football mad! On Saturday 8 January 1949 Yeovil, the only non-league team in the FA Cup Third Round, would take on 2nd Division Bury at the Huish ground.

A record crowd was expected – and during the week 'three public-spirited veteran supporters', glove manufacturer Edwin 'Tink' Robbins, Supporters Club Chairman 68 years old Ted Perrott, and retired brewery worker Ted Cooper, 71, laid dozens of railway sleepers and shovelled tons of earth to provide an extension for several hundred extra spectators on the Jubilee terrace. Hotels and guesthouses were full of national sports reporters and photographers, and camera teams from *Gaumont British News* were in town. Everything was ready for the big day, shops would shut, businesses close and the pubs had obtained special licences to open for two hours on the Saturday afternoon 'to give supporters an opportunity for celebrating.' (Remember this is 1949!)

They came from all across the West Country, in special trains, coaches, cars and on foot, filling the streets and were queuing outside the ground four hours before the 2 o'clock kick-off. The crowd of 13,500 ticket holders packed into every inch of the stand and terraces, others perched on buildings, advertisement hoardings and in trees overlooking the ground. In the stand was staunch supporter 86-years-old Mrs Minnie Gilham from West Coker who came into every home game and who, in the words of the *Western Gazette's* reporter, had 'A surprising knowledge of the game and who was fully aware of the financial difficulties besetting small non-league clubs – "Win or lose I'll still continue to organise my whist drives in the village for Yeovil FC," she declared.' Good luck messages were received from many of Yeovil's partners in the Southern League and from supporters in all parts of the country.

To a roar of approval, the Yeovil team, led by its 10-years-old mascot, Rex Rainey, ran onto the pitch and what happened next is football history. Player-manager Alec Stock's non-leaguers scored after seven minutes and never looked back defeating Bury 3-1. Yeovil's goals came from Jackie Hargreaves, Ray Wright and Bobby Hamilton.

At the final whistle, the crowd could contain themselves no longer and pouring onto the pitch carried the Yeovil team shoulder high to the dressing rooms. The *Western Gazette* reported that 'Ninety thrilling minutes put an end to any financial qualms the Club might have had. Their share of the gate, which amounted to nearly £700, doubled the existing bank balance. Three months ago the club feared an overdraft. Gross receipts were £1565.'

The result dropped the bookies odds on Yeovil winning the FA Cup from 5,000 – 1 against to 500 – 1 against.

Speaking after the game, Bury's manager. Norman Bullock told the *Gazette's* 'R.G.K.' that:

'Yeovil were easily the better side and thoroughly deserved to go into the next round. Their standard of play was far better than he had expected, and they backed it up by lots of confidence and great team spirit, When I asked him if the sloping pitch had played any part in Bury's downfall, Mr Bullock, the great sportsman that he is, replied: "I should be the last person to suggest that this had anything to do with Yeovil's success. They played the right type of football and deservedly won on their merit. I wish them the best of luck in the next round."'

Four supporters from Taunton wrote to the *Western Gazette's* Sports Editor expressing appreciation of the kindly co-operation of the residents of Queen Street whose back gardens adjoined one of the terraces. The Tauntonians had only a slender chance of seeing the game from the top of the packed terrace and 'asked two housewives over the garden wall if they could lend a stool. A chair and a stool were immediately forthcoming

– excellent "platform" accommodation. The Good Samaritans resolutely declined any security for their property, and also declined a token of appreciation when it was returned.'

The Yeovil 'giant-killers' were on their way to the Fourth Round of the FA Cup and next in their sights would be the 'mighty Sunderland.'

'YEOVIL ASTONISH FOOTBALL WORLD' cried the *Western Gazette* on 4 February 1949 and went on to tell how:

'Jubilant scenes reminiscent of V.E.-Day followed Saturday's sensational Fourth Round FA Cup-tie by Yeovil Town's £100-a-week team of part-time professionals over Sunderland, a club which has never been out of the First Division and whose players cost over £60,000 in transfer fees. The town went wild with excitement and people who thronged the streets demonstrated their delight, forgetting their accustomed southern reserve. The celebrations were by no means confined to the town for wherever Somerset folk gathered the sole topic of conversation was Yeovil's success. There was for instance a terrific cheer when on the stage of the Pavilion Theatre at Bournemouth came a member of the cast wearing a huge green and white rosette, who laughingly commentated: "Roses are red and violets are blue, Sunderland one, Yeovil two."'

The Cup fever which had gripped Yeovil during the weeks leading up to the match on 29 January had resulted in an overwhelming demand for tickets even though the price of a seat in the stand had gone up to 10s.6d., and the enclosure to 7s.6d.; however, the ground tickets were held at two shillings but with no concessions to Supporters Club members or schoolboys. Everyone wanted a ticket and in the words of the Yeovil Club Secretary '35,000 people want to obtain admission to a ground which is limited to 15,000'.

On 21 January, the *Western Gazette* reported that:

'Extraordinary scenes were witnessed at the ground on Tuesday when applicants for a limited number of ground tickets began queuing in the morning. First there was Mrs Beatrice Beacham, of 59 Garden City, Langport, who arriving at 11 am, waited eight hours to obtain a ticket for her 18-years-old son who plays for the Langport team. Hundreds who waited throughout the afternoon, including elderly women and children, were served with tea by women members of the Supporters Club. Trouble brewed in the early evening when factory workers swarmed into the ground from all directions, and people who had been waiting in the queue for several hours found themselves in a milling and jostling crowd of 2000 with no hope of obtaining tickets. There were angry scenes and cat-calls as a section of the crowd made a rush for the ticket office and police reinforcements had to be sent to the ground. When the police and Club officials were finding difficulty in holding the angry and disappointed crowd in check, Supt. F. B. Hanham made a timely intervention and appealed to them to go home quietly. "I am disgusted and ashamed," he said. "I have seen occurrences like this in other towns but I never thought it could happen at Yeovil." The Superintendent promised some hope for disappointed supporters when he said: "If the ground capacity should be extended and more tickets are printed I will do what I can to help everyone to get a square deal."

The *Western Gazette* went on to refer to trouble outside a couple of evening newspaper offices when their allocation of tickets was sold out within 20 minutes.

However, the problems of the tickets had evaporated by the big day as the crowd began to form outside the ground at eight o'clock and by the time the gates opened at noon, the queue stretched, six deep, for nearly half a mile along Huish, through Clarence Street and into The Park. Fog delayed many of the 1000 or so Sunderland supporters, who travelled the 400 miles from County Durham to Yeovil by road and rail, until after the kick-off. A coach party from a Sunderland working men's club who found themselves without accommodation following a booking mix up were rescued by Yeovil Labour Club whose members found overnight rooms for the visitors.

Over 17,000 ticket holders were finally packed into the Huish ground, whilst the ticketless watched from the windows and roofs of adjoining houses, the brewery buildings overlooking the ground from nearby Clarence Street or listened to the BBC commentary relayed from police car radios.

Resplendent in their new strip of green and white presented by the ladies section of the Supporters Club and with the town's coat of arms on their shirts, the Yeovil team ran onto the pitch to a deafening roar from the crowd and after tearing into Sunderland for 26 minutes, player-manager Alec Stock placed the ball in the back of the visitor's net – Yeovil 1 Sunderland 0. Fifteen minutes into the second half Sunderland equalised but inspired defending and constant attacking by Yeovil forwards kept the score level and the game went into extra time. By now the atmosphere was electric and the emotion released 14 minutes later when Yeovil's Eric Bryant scored could almost be seen. Alec Stock's team held on for the remaining 15 minutes and at the final whistle, Yeovil was in the Fifth Round of the FA Cup.

In the Club's boardroom after the match, Sunderland's Chairman, Colonel 'Joe' Prior, raised his glass to his hosts and said:

'You have won the game deservedly, your's are a grand lot of lads and their splendid team spirit won them the match. If in the next round you are again drawn at home and you play as you did today you will go a long way in the Cup. A lot has been said about your ground but I like it. In all my years of football I have never experienced such a warm welcome as I have had at Yeovil and although we have lost – it will be a shock to the folk back home – it has been well worth it to find such friendship and hospitality. My only regret is that we were unable to force a draw and repay your kindness at Roker Park.'

Yeovil's record-breaking Cup run was not over and next on the list was the legendry MANCHESTER UNITED!.

Yeovil's win against the 'mighty Sunderland' and entry into the Fifth Round of the FA Cup brought congratulations at the rate of several hundred a day from across the country, from West Country emigrants in Australia, South Africa and Canada, supporters in Sweden, Switzerland and Germany and from Servicemen in garrisons around the world. The Mayor, Alderman Ben Dening, received a midnight telephone call from the News Editor of the *Ontario Star* telling him how his readers had been thrilled by Yeovil's success and wanting to know all about the town and its winning team.

Yeovil was drawn to play the winners of the replay between Bradford and Manchester United and on the 4th February the waiting was over – it would be the Cup holders and 7 – 2 favourites Manchester United away at Maine-road on 12 February. Yeovil's Chairman, Bert Smith was delighted with the result commenting that, 'It is the best draw we could have wished for and we are assured of the biggest gate of at least 80,000.'

Players and officials of the 'Giant Killing' Yeovil Town Football Club.

Cup-tie fever raged through the town with many factories and businesses deciding to make the trip to Manchester as their annual outing and one glove factory booked a special train for its 600 employees. Special trains were laid on by British Rail with the Manchester return fare at 37s.6d. (£1.85) and dozens of coaches were hired to make the 250-mile journey.

'R.G.K.' of the *Western Gazette,* who was travelling with the team, described their departure: 'Engine whistles shrieked and detonators exploded on the line as the gaily bedecked train in green and white pulled out from Pen Mill Station yesterday (Thursday) morning taking Yeovil Town's team of part-time professional footballers to meet the holders Manchester United at Maine-road tomorrow (Saturday) in the 5th Round of the FA Cup. Will Yeovil's team of players drawn from factory, workshop and office make modern soccer history, by being the first non-league club to reach the 6th Round of the competition? This was the question uppermost in the minds of the crowd who gave them a resounding send-off. There were cheers, too, from the many early morning workers, as they arrived at the station to catch their buses to local factories.

'Before the team left, a portable wireless was presented by Mr J. Hart, a gift which Mr Hart had promised the Chairman if the team beat Sunderland in the last round of the Cup.

'At the last minute several players rushed from the train to fetch the crate of eggs and sherry, the match winning tonic, which had somehow been overlooked.

'News of the team's departure spread all along the line, and I saw groups of people lining wayside stations where "Good Luck" slogans appeared overnight.'

The supporters, including the mayor, left for the north by road and rail in what was described as the biggest exodus the town had ever known and over 3000 fans on six special trains set off late Friday for the overnight journey to Manchester.

Although the February sky was grey and cold, the welcome the Yeovil team and its supporters received in Manchester could not have been warmer. At Lewis's Market Street Department Store, with seating for 2000, Yeovil supporters were offered special breakfasts, lunches and teas to keep out the cold and hotels made available wash and brush-up facilities for the fans after their long overnight journey.

From the time the Yeovil team arrived in the city they were feted and 'R.G.K.' recounted how they were, 'Idolised by a Cup-frenzied populace. Besieged by admirers and autograph hunters in the streets, stores and in theatres and cinemas they many times had to seek police aid.'

Hundreds of messages of support reached the team in their hotel, including one from Gloversville in the USA. 'R.G.K.' could hardly contain himself as he reported that:

'Six thousand West Country fans brought colour and noise to a drab Manchester on Saturday morning. With rattles, bells, motor horns and a drum, they told the city that theirs was no small town team. They even brought a special Yeovil-made glove in green and white with an 18-inch span and two and a half feet long. Out rivalled only by Wembley were the amazing scenes at Maine-road. All gates were closed 20 minutes before the kick-off, when it was estimated that there were 80,000 in the ground. (The gate was 81,565) Thousands were locked out.

'One hour before the match was due to commence many of the gates on the popular side were closed. So dense was the crowd inside that several hundred youngsters were passed over the heads of waiting onlookers and were allowed to sit inside the wall behind the touch line. Thousands of

Soccer fans had queued in crowded Manchester Piccadilly for 'buses which moved off at the rate of one every 30 seconds.'

As for the match, Yeovil's part-timers had no real hope against the Cup holders with six internationals on the field playing before their home crowd, and the defeat of 8-0 was not unexpected. However Yeovil fought gallantly and United's Manager, the great Matt Busby, said that Alec Stock's team had 'played hard and never gave up trying – their display was a credit to non-league clubs'. Manchester's Vice-Chairman, Harold Hardman, praised the team in no uncertain terms, 'It has been the most sporting game we have seen at Maine-road this season. Yeovil have left a lasting impression.'

Thus Yeovil's dreams of Cup glory ended but the team and its supporters could look back on an exciting few weeks in the drab winter of 1949 and a place in football history.

10

BRIDGWATER'S FIFTH OF NOVEMBER CARNIVAL

Bridgwater is justly proud (and so is Somerset) of its November Illuminated Carnival which attracts tens of thousands of people from across the West Country and overseas. The roots of the carnival can be traced back to the discovery of the Gun Powder Plot in November 1605 the story of which is too well known to be repeated and the subsequent celebrations involving the burning of the effigy of Guy Fawkes.

From the early 1600s Bridgwater celebrated the event with a massive bonfire at the Cornhill, and which over the succeeding years became more and more elaborate involving costumes, music and the illuminated carnival procession. Local people who dressed up and took part became known as Masqueraders. One of the main features of the carnival is the 'squibbing' when the procession ends, the 'squibs' being a firework held aloft at the end of a long pole by the 'Squibber' standing in a line in the town centre.

The first modernised illuminated carnival appeared on 5 November 1881 lit by oil lamps and electric lighting was introduced in 1931.

In its publication of 7 November 1900, reproduced below, the *Taunton Courier* describes the first Bridgwater Carnival of the twentieth century:

'Bridgwater, without its Fifth of November Carnival, would hardly be Bridgwater. This popular function was again held in the town on Monday evening, and passed off very successfully in spite of the uncertain weather.

'Bridgwater has two heroes – Robert Blake and Guy Fawkes – and it is not easy to say offhand which of the two it holds in higher honour than the other. Blake, it is true, was a native of the town, but this circumstance, until quite recently, seemed to be regarded locally as a distinction that the town had conferred on Blake rather than *vice versa*. On the other hand, it had never been alleged that Guy Fawkes had the remotest connection with Bridgwater; he probably had never even heard of its existence. This probably is the reason why year after year, as long as the oldest inhabitant can remember and longer, while Blake's memory was perpetrated in a paragraph by the local historian, the Bridgwater people have celebrated with ever-increasing zeal the anniversary of the greatest pyrotechnical display which Mr Fawkes organised at Westminster for the benefit of King James I and his Parliament. Nor even now, has their enthusiasm at all abated, and if Blake's statue on the Cornhill stood in the way of the Fifth of November Carnival bonfire, so much the worse for the statue. As a matter of fact, it had to be protected on Monday night by a covering of wet tarpaulins. The bonfire, be it remembered, is no small affair. It is a huge, flaming, smoking mountain of tar barrels, the red reflection of which lights up the sky for miles around, as if the whole town were afire, and from early evening till early morning it burns on, with an insatiable appetite for combustibles, surrounded all the time by dense crowds of people who are constantly agitated by the approach of some gang of masqueraders indiscriminately squibbing everyone within reach. Yet no accident beyond such as are unavoidable in large crowds ever occurs, and this is the marvel of it all. Either the carnival is extraordinarily well organised or the town is extraordinarily lucky. The weather is a factor which is not of much account in these carnivals; they are held in almost any weather and the masqueraders, of whom there are thousands of all ages, require to be thoroughly drenched before their enthusiasm is at all damped. Not much anxiety was felt, therefore about the weather, though it was distinctly inclined to be wet. The town was full of visitors, who had come not only from the neighbouring villages, but even many from Bristol, Taunton and Weston to witness the unique celebration. About six o'clock the procession, which has always been one of the great features of the carnival began to be marshalled near the Great Western Railway Station. The first division was headed by the Fire Brigade and the familiar effigy of Guy Fawkes, with his lantern, which has led the van on many occasions, but looked none the worse for wear. In the Chairman's carriage sat Mr S. M. J. Woods, the popular Somerset cricketer who, since he became president, has done much to improve the organisation of the carnival. Next was the statue of William Blake who was capitally represented by Mr G.

J. White who successfully assumed the commanding attitude in which the sculptor has portrayed the great sea warrior. The "Handy Man" was a striking tableau showing Britannia surrounded by a group of Jack Tars in charge of a 4.7 gun, a pom-pom and a searchlight – an effective and well-mounted scene. A company of Court messengers of Louis XV's period made a brave show in their handsome costumes. A Red Cross knight in chain armour and mounted was also an imposing figure. A gang of clowns amused the public on the way, and the softer sex was represented by the "Blue Bell Beauties" girls in blue and white costumes. Division II was led by the Taunton Band. The siege of Mafeking was realistically depicted in a tableau that followed. There was a picture of a little town on the veldt with its defenders behind their sand-bag entrenchments. Behind came a Boer commando and Colonel Mahon's relief force. General Baden-Powell was, of course, a striking central figure. Cyrano and his Gascon gang were certainly one of the best groups of masqueraders. From Weston-super-Mare came a contingent of masqueraders, who took part in the procession, noticeably among there being John Bull jun. a little boy on a bicycle whose appearance was very amusing, The Swift's Football Club was followed by the Bristol Medical football team, who looked none the worse for the licking that Bridgwater had given them in the afternoon. For Division III the Burnham Fife and Drum Band made things lively, and prepared the way for the grand old patriotic tableau, "Sons of the Empire." It represented Britannia surrounded by John Bull, a Scotch lassie, a Welsh girl, and an Irishman, in their local costumes, led by her Colonial sons, together with the leaders of the British Army in South Africa – Lord Roberts, General Buller, Lord Kitchener and others. It was a most effective scene and aroused much enthusiasm. Numerous other masqueraders brought up the rear of the procession. The tail was composed of local take-offs which evidently had a humourous significance. Several trades were as usual represented in the procession. Collections were made for a local charity were made *en route*. It is also a moot point whether the procession was as good as in past years. On this occasion however, it was generally agreed that it might be classed with the best of them in point of brilliance and variety, and it was certainly better lighted than usual. Later in the evening the principal gangs took part in a squib display contest in the High-street and only those who know what the Bridgwater squibs are like can imagine the fiery spectacle which the combined displayed afforded. It was not only in the principal streets that all the fun took place; many of the side streets had their bonfires and almost every child old enough to toddle was dressed up by his proud parents in some fanciful costumes, and allowed to set off a few crackers from the doorstep. The whole town was enveloped in flame and smoke, and emerged as usual, unscathed.'

In 1900, the British Empire was at its peak, but in South Africa, a very nasty war was being fought by the Empire against the two Boer (Afrikaner) republics, the South African Republic and the Orange Free State. The war lasted from October 1899 until May 1902 with the British victory. In the November 1900 carnival procession, a number of the tableaux featured incidents from the war and some of the British commanders.

Squibbing at Bridgwater's fifth of November Carnival.

11

CYCLING IN 1930

THE YEOVIL CYCLING Club was founded on 31 May 1928 by a few enthusiastic cyclists under the Chairmanship of Mr R. F. Hancock, with Mr F Coram as Hon Secretary; the first year's membership was 29 and Club funds £2.

The club's first Handbook was published in 1931 the current Chairman being Mr D. Chapman, and in his Introduction he wrote how the club 'Has grown from a few fellows, whose sole interest was riding, to a band of "Lads and Lassies" who Ride, Race, Ramble, Swim, Sing and Dance.'

During the first year, a Racing Section was started, in February 1930 the club became affiliated to the Road Racing Council, and the club's Open events were given 'official status'.

The club headquarters in 1931 was at the Railway Tavern on Middle Street (The William Dampier now stands on the site), and club runs were held on Sundays, starting in Westminster Street. Racing and time trials were popular, and the 1930 season 'was notable for the appearance of Ladies for the first time in the club's history'. A social meeting was held on the first Monday of each month at 7.30 pm, and at 31 December 1930, the membership was 56 and club funds £10.

'SPOKE' gave a summary of all the Sunday runs held from 22 June to 16 November 1930, a few of which are described in the rest of this chapter.

The first was on 22 June. '8 Members started out for an all day run to Bridport, via Weymouth, Abbotsbury, and Swyre. Tea at the Tiger Inn, Bridport, and the journey totalled 86 miles.

'6th July (Sunday). Three members were out for an all night run to Lynmouth, and returned to the Market House Inn, Bridgwater, where 9 others were met for Tea. The 9 members had a ramble over the Quantock Hills covering 90 miles, whilst the all night riders had covered about

170 to 180.

'20th July (Sunday). An afternoon run was arranged to Lyme Regis. Seven members turned out, and Tea was served at the Cottage Hotel. The weather on this run left much to be desired, in fact, it was so wet and rough that although H.M.S. *Rodney* was in Lyme the Naval authorities would allow no visitors to the Ship, and no sailors on land. About 50 miles.

'10th August (Sunday). Lulworth Cove, Tea at the Isis Hotel, Weymouth. Five members were out, and covered about 75 miles.

'7th September (Sunday). A ramble in Devon Lanes, calling at Seaton and Beer, Tea at the Hare and Houses, Whitford. Some members indulged in a little bathing, and when ready for departure, found their clothes a little damp, much to their discomfort. 75 miles were covered by this run.

'14th September (Sunday). Eleven members were out for an afternoon run to Farnham, via Blandford, where tea was arranged at the Museum Hotel. About 70 miles were covered, and quite a good number of these in very hard rain.

'21st September (Sunday). All day run, five members turning out for a rather exciting run, with the exception of a mishap at Brean Down near

Weymouth was a popular destination of the Yeovil Cycling Club.

Weston. A return was made to Bridgwater for Tea at the Market House Inn, and this run was about 80 miles.

'5th October (Sunday). This was our end of the Season Rally to the Hare and Hounds at Whitford, and 25 members were out. 56 miles.

'19th October (Sunday). An all day ramble over the Quantock Hills. 8 members were out for this Run covering 92 miles, and Tea was arranged at the Market House, Bridgwater, where they were met by two other members, who had earlier that day more or less lost themselves on "Top o' the Mendips." Serve them right!

'26th October (Sunday). A rather slow all day run (against the wind) to Dorchester, Abbotsbury, The Hardy Monument, and Swyre, then to the Tiger Inn, Bridport for tea. This was an expensive trip for one or two members who did a bit of rough riding around the Hardy Monument district. We escaped however with only one broken fork. 70 miles.

'16th November (Sunday). An afternoon run to Bathpool, eight members turning out for tea at the Bathpool Arms (where was the Chairman today?) I believe there was the Christening of his "Sun."

The last run for 1930 was on Sunday 30 November when 'One member out all day around Blandford and Shaftesbury, where 11 others turned up for Tea at "Ye Olde Two Brewers." What was it one member stepped on the gas for when a sudden thought struck him? The record remains silent. The last run totalled 92 miles.'

12

MARTOCK'S PATRIOTIC ENTHUSIASM IN JUNE 1900

On 12 October 1899, following years of tension in South Africa, war broke out between the Boer Republics of Transvaal and the Orange Free State and Great Britain. Within a short time, the Boers had the British forces bottled up in Kimberley, Ladysmith and Mafeking, and for many months bloody battles would be fought as our army sought to raise the sieges and defeat the Boers. As the weeks passed the news got gloomier following reverse after reverse as the Imperial forces struggled to break through to the towns, and back at home large reinforcements of regular and volunteer troops were being gathered and sent south. During the first six months of 1900, the tide of war finally turned in Britain's favour, and the sieges were raised. When the Boer's capital of Pretoria was surrendered to the British army on 5 June 1900, it seemed that at last the war was over, and there was general rejoicing.

Even back in 1900, news travelled fast. At 11.40 am on 5 June, the British Commander in Chief, Lord Roberts (Bobs) sent an official telegram to the Government notifying them of the Boer surrender, and within two hours the news was flashed around the country. What followed its receipt in Martock was described two days later on 7 June in *Palmer's Weekly News*, Martock's own newspaper, first published on Thursday 15 March 1883 by Mr Montrose Addison Palmer from his house in Water Street and which continued without a break for another 34 years until 19 July 1917:

'The Church bells at once rang out merrily (though they were ringing before because it was Club day, but even bells can be rung merrily and merrier), flags were displayed from almost every house in the place. Sparrow's factory hooter again sounded forth and for miles round told of the day's events; cannons were fired and men paraded in the streets in burlesque costume. The Vicar, assisted by the Field Marshall, Mr Walter Palmer, and others arranged for an evening demonstration which was carried out on even a more elaborate scale than that of the Relief of Mafeking, the Female Benefit Society very loyally consenting to forego their evening dance in the Schoolroom so that their Band may head the procession. The assembly took place in Church Street at 8.30. The Field Marshall, well-mounted and fully equipped, was now escorted by a dozen splendid horses carrying gallant Englishmen ready at any time for any emergency. Two army men, Private C. Ring (in Khaki) and Private Mark Rowland (Royal Army Medical Corps), both invalided home from the "front," took part in the demonstration. The procession was smartly formed up headed by the flag of "Love and Unity," and the CLB Band (under Bandmaster Mr A. E. Worner), then came the Naval Brigade, CLB, Members of the Female Benefit Society, Fire Brigade with Engine, Oddfellows and Foresters (in regalia), Males' Benefit Society, and a whole caravan of decorated vehicles of various descriptions, full of employees of the industries of the town, and others, representing a spectacle never here surpassed and rarely equally elsewhere. Among the fancy costumes was represented the bonny Scotch laddie in full dress and another unit of note was the Proprietor of the Hurst Bakery

The procession celebrating the Boer surrender marched up through North Street.

bearing the "staff of life." The Band led the National Anthem, all joining in, and the start was made. The route taken was through Water Street to the top of Hinton and back, then through North Street to the Station & back. Most houses were illuminated, and cheers were given at several residences en route. The Committee were very reluctant to curtail the route of the procession by not passing through East Street, and also round the top of Hinton and through Middle Street where much time had been spent in putting up splendid decorations, and also especially for not halting at the Railway Hotel where Mr White, with his usual generosity, had prepared a most hospitable reception. The sole reason was to spare the Band as much as possible. They had a heavy week in hand, and after two days clubs it was very good of them to lead as they did, a march round Hinton being very tiring. Returned to Church Street, the Field Marshall addressing the throng in inspiring and patriotic language eloquently eulogized the splendid work done by Lord Roberts and his Staff in maintaining in so capable a manner the prestige of our Empire. On his call rounds of cheers were given for "Bobs" as only Martock "Beans" can do it, several ladies heartily joining in. Cheers were also given for our troops, the Vicar, the Field Marshall, and the Band. God Save the Queen closing a record gathering.'

Alas, the rejoicing was premature, the Boers were not defeated, and although they could never open up a major offensive as in the autumn of 1899, a savage guerrilla war was waged for the next two years, and peace would not be restored until May 1902.

13

THE *WESTERN GAZETTE* SPORTS AUGUST 1911

On Friday 25 August 1911, the *Western Gazette* wrote that; 'The members of the *Western Gazette* Athletic Club scored another brilliant success with their annual sports which were held in the Home Field, Newton, on Saturday, by kind permission of the Rev. E. H. Bates Harbin and Mr A. James. This is the tenth year in succession that the sports have been held, and the gratifying support which has been accorded by the townspeople has now established for them a sound position.'

The weather on Saturday 19 August was beautiful and the programme for the tenth annual sports was the largest with nearly 30 events. Over 4000 people enjoyed the sports, but it was reported that the strike on the railways had reduced the number of people coming to Yeovil from many of the surrounding towns and villages; a number of competitors were also unable to attend because of the lack of rail services.

The obstacle race at the Western Gazette *Sports.*

However, despite the travel problems, a great day was enjoyed by all who came to see the individual and team flat races, a five-mile marathon around the field, obstacle races, jumping, bicycle competitions, donkey races, a Donkey Musical Chairs race, skipping and skipping for skill contests, skittles, push ball and a keenly fought tug-of-war.

The *Western Gazette* reported that:

'Upwards of £50 in value was offered in prizes and four handsome challenge cups. The entries to all the events were exceedingly good and several had to be run in heats. The boys' races (under 16) attracted no fewer than 20 competitors, and all but one ran, the premier award being carried off by V. Hooper. Mr F. J. Hicks offered a magnificent cup in the one-mile bicycle race for championship of the district, and the scratch man J. Newman, proved a fine winner. The cup has to be won three years in succession to become the competitor's property. The handsome trophy offered by Mr J. Trevor-Davies to the winner of the Club obstacle race was finely won by E. A. Elliott, who did not seem to experience the difficulty as the other competitors in picking out the floating cork from a tub of water. Mr G. H. Gould offered a magnificent cup to be won outright for the championship of Yeovil in the quarter of a mile flat race, A. Priddle being the winner. The cup becomes his absolute property. Much interest was evinced in a Marathon race of five miles round the field, in which there were twelve starters. W. Warren of Wiveliscombe got away at the commencement, and maintained first place throughout, winning by nearly a lap over the second man.'

The tug-of-war was one of the main features of the *Gazette's* annual sports and the competition could be fierce. This year the teams entered were – Public Works, Tintinhull, Sherborne Territorials, Petters' United, Bird and Pippard and Stoford. Several teams from outside the district had been prevented from attending due to the rail strike. The winners were the Sherborne Territorials' team of Sergeant Foot (captain), Corporal Luck, Lance Corporals Park, Dowell and Plimpton and Privates W. Best, R. Best, Gillingham and Cox.

Another popular event was Push Ball in which Public Works were defeated by Yeovil Reserves and Petters' Infants accounted for Yeovil Dwarfs. Petters' Infants won the contest with each member of the winning team receiving a medal.

The day ended with an evening concert of songs, duets and instrumental items on the lawn of Newton Farm illuminated by fairy lights, and dancing in a large marquee to the Yeovil Town Band.

By the way, the skipping contest for skill was won by Dora Sibley, R. Giles was second, and Rosa Gay, third.

14

THE SOUTH SOMERSET MUSIC COMPETITION

THE SECOND SOUTH Somerset Musical Competition was held in Yeovil on 23, 24, and 25 April 1912 and the *Western Gazette* reported that the first competition had been held in Crewkerne in 1911 on the initiative of Miss Trask of Norton-sub-Hamdon 'whose musical activities are so well known'. One of the chief objects of the competition was to widen the sphere and knowledge of music. Chamber music was introduced into the 1912 programme, and had been the inspiration for the formation of the South Somerset Symphony Orchestra.

The orchestral theme of the 1912 competition was the work of Haydn, but a wide cross section of music, both vocal and orchestral, was performed. The entries came from the towns and villages of South Somerset and included schools, churches, choirs and instrumentalists. Contests took place in the Princes Street Assembly Rooms and the organ tests were held in St John's church. The judges were the Rev. Dr Davis, organist of Wells Cathedral, Dr E.T. Sweeting, Master of the Music, Winchester College, and Mr Harry Evans from Liverpool. The *Western Gazette* stated that the judges:

'Were painstaking in their duties, and their comments on the classes were to the point. As instancing their interest, an incident on Wednesday night is worth mention. East Chinnock Choral Society and Norton Church choir had sung "The Heavens are telling," and the performance of the former left much to be desired. At the suggestion of the judges, the choirs were combined, and the scant audience had the uncommon experience of seeing two village choirs, conducted by such a well known musician as Mr Harry Evans, who had as his band two doctors of music at the piano.'

The first day's contests were confined mainly to children and included the massed schools of Yeovil singing in the churchyard 'O England my

Country,' 'Heavenly Father send Thy Blessing' and the National Anthem. A brass quartet comprising Messrs Russell (trumpet), Chant (cornet) and Ring and Harris (trombones) accompanied the children, and Mr Hudson, seen standing on the cart in the picture, conducted. The *Western Gazette* noted that the children sang 'with great keenness'. On that first day, there were performances by Elementary School and Children's Choirs, Children's Action Songs, piano solos and duets, violin solos and duets, violins and pianos, and pianos, violins and cellos.

Contestants in the South Somerset Music Competition in St John's churchyard.

Adults performed on the second day when there were vocal soloists – soprano, mezzo-soprano, alto, contralto, tenor, baritone and bass; vocal duetists, and trios, village quartets, village choirs and organists.

The final day saw performances by male and female choirs, instrumental trios and quartets. string-quartets, madrigal singers and in the evening the South Somerset Symphony Orchestra, conducted by Miss Trask, played Haydn's 8th Symphony at a concert in the Town Hall.

The *Western Gazette* wrote that the 1913 competition would involve the works of Mozart, with Beethoven and modern writers following in future years. The paper commented hopefully that 'Although it is fully realised that there may be few visible results of the contest for some years, it is hoped that in this way, knowledge of the great wealth of musical literature may be gained.'

15

'DINAH MITE' AND 'THE FLAMINGO CLUB'

On 29th May 1953, the *Western Gazette* wrote enthusiastically about the show being presented by the St Peter's Youth Club.

'72 YOUNG PEOPLE IN
YEOVIL REVUE
St Peter's Youth Club
Stage "Dinah Mite"

'A revue which cannot fail to be a success is "Dinah Mite," Yeovil St Peter's Youth Club's third public production, which they presented last night (Thursday), at Summerleaze Park School. Further performances will be given tonight and tomorrow night.

'Strangely enough, the reasons why this show will get plenty of "credits" are not so much acting, singing or dancing ability – or these, as might be expected with a cast mainly composed of very young children, are limited – but really because of the 72 lively youngsters taking part is so infectious that enthusiasm and applause on the part of the audience come naturally.

'Local Script Writer
'"Dinah Mite" tells the hilarious story of a little girl from the day she won first prize in the baby show to the day she held a ball to celebrate her 21st birthday, writes our representative, who saw the dress rehearsal on Tuesday. Keith Burgess, who wrote the script, helped Mrs W.F. Clark with the production and also took a principal part, must be selected as the show's guiding genius. His script was excellently written, his humour incessant,

and his own burlesque as a vicar and a schoolmaster remarkably funny.

'Mrs Clark had a far from easy task in training to sing, dance and act in public more than 50 very young girls. Her policy, apparently was to get parts for every member of the youth club. The production on the whole was hall-marked by the irrepressible keenness of the younger performers.

'Principal Role

'"Dinah" was played by Gillian Pearce, a perky and coquettish little minx with a roguish twinkle in her eye. She had the knack of looking six years old when she was supposed to be, and also a very sophisticated 21 when the occasion demanded. Hers was the only real principal role and much of the continuity depended on her handling of the comic situations.

'Comic high spots were shared by Keith Burgess, Gillian Pearce and another excellent impromptu comedian, Ron Batty, who played Mrs Mite, in the best pantomime dame style, and "Billy Ous," a "dim" schoolboy. Jean White was a stately Lady Holman and June Williams a good caricature of a vicar's wife.

'Another "credit" for the company was the designing and making of all the scenery and the costumes in the show. Both these were specially effective, particularly the scenery, constructed by Mr H. J. Tompkins and Mr R. A. Batty. Mr H. J. B. Hughes, assisted by Keith Grant, was in charge of lighting effects. Other help was given by Mrs H. Tompkins and Mrs Cleal.

'Music was selected and played by Brenda Clark and Keith Tavener, and dances were arranged by Brenda Clark, Jean White and Pat White. Vocal solos, "On wings of song" by Mendelssohn, and "Friend of Mine," were sung by Jean White and Keith Tavener.

'The Cast

'Other parts were taken by Glenys Gould (Mrs Bee), Keith Clark (Horace Little), John Creek (Tom Atto), Michael Grinter (Percy Ponger), Derick Rendall (Paul Tall), and Pepe Turner (Gertrude) and Patricia White (Fairy Foxglove). Also in the cast were Doreen Cook, Gillian Elliott, Betty Fisk, Marian Austen, Pat Brophy, Roma Cleal, Joyce Greenwood, Jackie Matthews, Elizabeth Pocket, Sally Darke, Jean Farrant, Pauline Rice, Annett Rogers and David Devoto.

'Younger dancers and members of the chorus were: – Susan Hurford, Wendy Hall, Elizabeth Glover, Elizabeth Parker, Jennifer Elliott, Carol Shire, Susan Hill, Jeannette Fitzgerald, Eileen Tate, Cynthia Churchill, Marylin Miles, Kathleen Barnes, Florence Barnes, Rosemary Elliott, Hazel Tetlow, Denise Ralph, Janice Parker, Betty Windsor, Pat Grundy, Diane Elliott, Jackie Creese, Sheila Trott, Jean Barnes, Anne Tompkins, Janet Elford, Janet Neal, Valerie Whitewood. Junior Group – Jenny Darke, Jenny Amatt, Jenny White, Mary Prince, Jean Richards, Valerie Austen, Pauline Mountain, Joan Monhurl, Elaine Wells, Ann Knight, Carol Hyde, Margaret White, Pat Parker, Eileen Hyde, Ann Montacute, Mary Windsor, Stella Moore.'

Building on the 1953 success, the Club began the five-night run of their 1954 production 'The Flamingo Club,' on Tuesday 27 April in St Peter's Church Hall, Coronation Avenue, laid out to resemble a night club. The *Western Gazette* wrote that:

'The show produced by Mrs W. F. Clark, was of a high standard. As the music of the opening song sung by Miss Patricia Allen died away, the show commenced with a scene entitled "Under New Management" showing the various types of "customers" at the Flamingo Club. Keith Burgess, dressed in tartan kilt, acted the part of a mean Scotsman and his girl friend was played by Miss Pauline Price. Assisting Keith to provide many hilarious incidents in this scene were Miss Brenda Clark, Keith Clark, Miss Gillian Pearce, David Devoto, Pepe Turner and Miss June Williams. Members of the junior girls' section dressed in costumes representing flowers and glow-worms, presented a novelty song and dance routine entitled "The Flowers and the Worms," accompanied at the piano by Miss Brenda Clark. An excellent display of ballet dancing by Miss Pauline Rice and Miss Sheila Trott was a feature of the act. An unrehearsed item caused much mirth when Keith Burgess asked for four volunteers to go on the stage to answer what he described as "simple" questions. Members of the senior boys' section of the Club, Keith Burgess, David Devoto, John Goff, Keith Grant, Derrick Rendell and Pepe Turner did a very clever piece of miming to gramophone records and were deservedly encored. Other items were old-time dancing in period costume, Spanish dancing by Misses Gillian Pearce and Sally Darke, an exhibition of skipping and a vocal solo.'

In April 1955, the Youth Club opened their six-night run of the 'First Anniversary of the Flamingo Club' in St Peter's Church Hall, with a large cast of 80 young people whose ages ranged from three to 19, and once again the show took the form of a cabaret in a night club.

'The opening scene, inside the Flamingo Club, to the music of Flamingo, with the original "customers" – Keith Clark and Brenda Clark as two American tourists, Keith Burgess as a mean Scotsman with his girl friend Jean Synick, and Gillian Pearce and David Devoto – brought back many pleasing memories for those who saw the first Flamingo production last year', wrote the *Western Gazette*, whose contributor went on to report that – 'Accent this year was on choreography and was a striking feature. The dance sequences were made even more effective by the expert way Keith Grant operated the lights to blend with the colourful costumes and scenery. Outstanding was the transformation of the Flamingo setting with a large artificial anniversary cake with one candle in the background, into an underwater scene for a sea ballet. Comedy also played a big part, and the audience was quick to appreciate natural comedian Keith Burgess.

The cast of 'Dinah Mite'.

'In an unrehearsed item, "What's My Line?" in which four members of the club impersonated well-known panel game celebrities, were asked to guess what four members of the audience would like to have been. Glenis Gould of the senior girls section, raised many laughs with her interpretation of a charwoman. Miming to gramophone records by members of the Boys' club also proved popular. '

'Vocal soloists were Carol Blacker and Heather Williams and Gillian Pearce and June Williams, and Sally Darke and Jean Farrant sang duets.

The show was produced by the leader of the girls' club, Mrs C. Clark. Script was by Miss Brenda Clark and Mr Keith Burgess; choreography, senior members of the girls' club; costumes, members of the girls' club, parents and friends; scenery Mr R. Gillham; lighting Mr Keith Grant; stage manager Mr C. Clark; assistant stage manager Mr B. Hurford; Catering arrangements were undertaken by Mrs H. Cleal, Mrs S. Pearce and Mrs B. Gundry.

'Taking part were: Susan Darke, Carol Ward, Evelyn Cavall, Elizabeth Glover, Cynthia Churchill, Carol Shire, Susan Crouch, Elizabeth Parker, Marlene Miles, Susan Herford, Heather Kane, Diane Beaton, Kathleen Barnes, Diana Way, Jennifer Creek, Susan Corbett, Margaret Cross, Margaret Way, Jennifer Whitewood, Pauline Montacute, Denise Beaton and Geraldine Beaton (junior girls club).

'Carol Blacker, Sylvia Gillham, Rita Melhuish, Jenny Darke, Marlene Clements, Gillian Horlock, Celia Galliott, Anne Gillham, Julia Williams, Julia Rowlands, Anne Montacute, Anne Hayward, Elaine Wills, Jenny White, Pat Parker, Dawn Harrison, Jenny Ammatt, Valerie Austin, Pauline Kane, Margaret Gaylard, Margaret Featherstone, Ann Robins, Denise Alder, Joan Monroe, Norma Singleton, Mary Pearce, Florence Barnes (intermediate girls' club).

'June Williams, Pat Miles, Jean Farrant, Janice Parker, Glenis Gould, Margaret White, Jackie Crease, Brenda Clark, Jean Synick, Valerie Whitewood, Roma Cleal, Doreen Cook, Ann French, Mary Leonard, Gillian Pearce, Sally Dark, Denise Ralph, Betty Montacute, Bridget White, Sheila Trott, Margaret Hill, Marion Austin and Heather Williams (senior girls' club).

'Pepe Turner, Keith Clark, John Goff, Derrick Rendall, Keith Grant, Keith Burgess and David Devoto (boys' club).'

16

KISSING IN SOMERSETSHIRE AND A FEW SOMERSET SAYINGS

On 15 August 1906 'JVS' sent a postcard called KISSING IN SOMERSET, one of a series about old English customs, to a Miss Crossman, of Westbury, Wiltshire, and this is what it said:

'It is an interesting study that of tracing the history of old customs of various places. Some of them are undoubtedly of great antiquity, such as the Flower Show at Taunton, the origin is put down by some to the time of King Arthur and the Druids. Somersetshire customs have very much struck the attention of strangers who find in difficult to account for such a difference in adjacent localities. A Cockney who has lately been "doing" Somerset made a note of the following peculiarities in regards kissing in the different parts of the County. Clevedon girls keep quite still till they are

The very pleasant old English custom.

well kissed, and then say "I think you ought to be ashamed." Highbridge girls when kissed close their eyes in ecstacy, and do not open them again until the process ceases. Bristol ladies on being kissed suggest a walk to Keynsham, where they expect a little more of it. At Wellington, the ladies receive a salute with Christian meekness and follow the Scriptural rule – when kissed on one cheek, they turn the other also. A Taunton girl, when kissed at once proposes a walk to Vivary Park. The Burnham girls act decidedly on the give and take principle, and object to being under any obligation. A Wiveliscombe girl on being kissed proposes a night visit to some neighbouring Druidical remains, some ancient inscriptions on which are considered to have talismanic power in influencing her dreams and future destiny. A Glastonbury girl insists on giving a return after four kisses. When a lady at Wells is kissed she blushes and says nothing. The ladies at Weston-super-Mare on being kissed smiles and simpers, puts on her hat and coat and proposes a visit to the Café, and have tea, junket and syllabubs in the romantic woods. A Bridgwater girl, while you are kissing her, falls in your arms and sighs aloud, *"O! how nice – do it again."* Minehead girls say "Now if you go kissing me 'Ma' will hear, but if I make the gate creak kiss me then, and she will not know the difference."

No mention of South Somerset ladies, perhaps they didn't! Reading this little treatise of a hundred years ago what is so striking is how innocent it all seems – it was another world.

And now a few old Somerset sayings together with their explanations from the *Somerset Year Book* of 1922

Bedlam Wind

Bedlam (at South Brewham) had the reputation of being a bleak place. It was said that a bellows-maker of some eighty years ago, one John Chamberlain, was in the habit of going there to get the wind to put in his bellows, hence their good quality.

Cadbury Funeral

When a deceased person is not greatly regretted by his relatives, or when the friends are likely to mark the occasion by festivities, Castle Cary people remark: 'Ah that'll be a Cadbury Funeral – dry eyes and wet droats!'

Fleas Arrive on March 1st

This is a common belief in certain parts of the county. At Yeovil it is said that on that date they come marching down Hendford Hill, and at Crewkerne similarly down Cemetery Hill! Housewives should be very careful to sweep their front door steps early on this morning, as they may thus drive away the inquisitive beasts.

Little Cup Makers

A nick-name for people of Wincanton. Sweetman has recorded what he believed to be a 'very old legend.' The story goes that once on a time a traveller was going along a high road in this neighbourhood, when he heard a loud cry from a ditch: 'Help, help, please pull me out.' The traveller stopped and enquired 'Who are you?' when he received the reply 'The liddle cup maker o' Wincanton.' 'Then stay where bist,' retorted the other 'If thee'd bin a *big*-cup maker I'd a helped thee, but a liddle-cup maker, never!'

Langport Men are jocularly reputed to be web-footed. This is no doubt attributed to the low lying and marshy nature of the surrounding country, which during the winter months is often under water.

Market Towns

Rhymes similar to the following are no doubt found in several parts of the county:-

> Hadspen, Honeywick, Pitcombe and Cole,
> Higher Shep'n, Lower Shep'n, Stoke and Knowl,
> Higher Zeals, Lower Zeals, Wolverton and Penn,
> There bain't twelve zich market-towns in England again.

Nick-Names

In the same way that Somerset people are sometimes called 'Cuckoo-penners,' the inhabitants of certain towns and villages have been given names, complimentary or otherwise, by their neighbours. Many of these have interesting stories behind them, but in many cases the reasons for the appellations have been entirely lost.

Here is a short list:-

Barton Rats
Beckington Bees
Burrow Hounds
Charlton Bulldogs
Cary Chickens
Chewton Bunnies
Crewkerne Moon-douters
Curry Clowns
Frome Dumbledores
Keinton Mice
Kingweston Candlesticks
Lyng Long-dogs
Langport Ducks
Road Wopses
Ruishot Cheats
Stoke Bulldogs
Stoke Pero Candlesticks
Wincanton Little Cup Makers
Wellington Roundheads

And finally Zummerzet.

The following verse contains every letter in the alphabet:

> Zome talk of purty Devonshire,
> Zome Cornwall grant the best;
> Ax me, I say that Zummerset's
> Just Queen of all the rest.

17

THE END OF THE SECOND WORLD WAR

VE-Day 8 May 1945
At the beginning of May 1945, the announcement of the defeat of Nazi Germany was expected at any time, and across the nation, arrangements were underway to celebrate Victory in Europe – VE-Day – when it arrived. Already Yeovil had prepared its programme of events, and the pubs had been granted extended opening hours to 11.30, pm for the great day.

Monday 7 May was an odd sort of day because everybody seemed to be waiting for something to happen and for Mr Churchill, The Prime Minister, to tell the nation that the war was over in Europe, but nothing happened. Then suddenly at 7.40 pm, the BBC announced in a news flash that the Prime Minister would broadcast to the nation at 3 o'clock on the next afternoon and that Tuesday 8 May would be Victory in Europe Day and a holiday; Wednesday would also be a holiday.

During that Monday evening the film with the strangely prophetic title *And Now Tomorrow* was showing in Yeovil's Odeon cinema when the news flash was announced and the audience stood on their seats and cheered.

VE-Day dawned in Yeovil with flags and streamers decorating the town centre, and a good-humoured crowd soon thronged the streets. Many were wearing red, white and blue ribbons, but were out-done by an elderly man who strode about wearing a top hat and a frock coat festooned with Union Jacks. All the town's churches and chapels threw open their doors and the noontime services were packed with worshippers. The Boys' and Girls' Brigades, led by their Band, marched through the streets following a service in the South Street Baptist Church.

At 3 o'clock, Winston Churchill announced in his long awaited broadcast, that the hostilities in Europe had officially ceased and an hour later the Mayor, Councillor William Vosper, standing on a platform built on the 1941 bomb site opposite the present HSBC Bank, addressed a jubilant crowd in the Borough.

The mayor recounted the events since the war began in September 1939, and paid tribute to the nation's fighting forces and our allies during the past five and a half years. In conclusion, he reminded everyone that the war was still going on in the Far East against the Japanese, and he hoped that when the final victory was won, the world could look forward to a long era of peace and prosperity. As the Mayor ended his speech, the bells of St John's church rang out a victory peal, and the people of Yeovil danced in the Borough or marched with arms linked through the town.

The mayor spoke again in the Borough at 7 o'clock, in the evening, and called upon Yeovilians to 'Sing and dance, for this is Victory Day – I want you to enjoy yourselves – well done Yeovil, we can be proud of ourselves!'

Now let the *Western Gazette* recall that May evening of 76 years ago:.

Celebrating VE-Day in the Borough.

'The scenes at Yeovil on the night of VE-Day were unequalled on any occasion within memory. The mood of the crowd was one of unrestrained jubilation. Hundreds whirled around in fantastic dances, jitterbugging, laughing, singing and shouting. Music was played by Bill Kelly and his Band and relayed through amplifiers on a National Fire Service van. Scores linked arms and marched vociferously through the streets. When dusk fell the lights in the streets blazed in the Borough, while in Sidney Gardens and Bide's Garden, high powered lamps strung among the trees gave theatrical beauty to the foliage and flower beds. In the centre of the town St John's grey walls that had withstood bombs in 1941, although some of the windows were damaged, were floodlit. Crowds gathered there, seeking the sense of quietude and peace that were to be found only a stone's throw from the joyous shouts and whirling thousands in the Borough. Tired momentarily with dancing and hoarse from shouting, they lay at ease on the floodlit grass.

'A cheer rent the air as the floodlights were turned on, then the revelry was renewed. The noise of fireworks and thunder flashes mingled with the music and the songs. Hour by hour the crowd thickened. The V.A.D. Somerset/19 members patrolled the town, and several girls who had danced in rings until they were giddy and fainted were revived – only to begin again.

'On and on the band played on and on the dancers danced. Midnight struck. The band had played non-stop since the early evening. They played until they could play no more. The crowd gave them a ringing cheer as they laid down their instruments after the singing of "Auld Lang Syne" and "God Save the King."

'The band went home, but the crowd didn't. From nowhere appeared an accordian and hundreds at a time gathered round the single minstrel. Outside the Westminster Bank a large crowd gathered and dancing went on for nearly two hours. Cheering people marched through the streets right up to 3.30 am. It was a night to remember!'

At 10.15 in the morning of VE-Day plus One, the 9 May, crowds lined the streets and cheered the mile-long parade of over a thousand men and women of the three fighting services, Civil Defence, and the United States Army, as led by three bands, they marched from Sherborne Road to the Huish Football Ground for the Public Thanksgiving Service. Many thousands of townspeople gathered in and around the Huish Ground, and there was cheering and warm applause as the US Army contingent marched in led by Sergeant C. W. Whitaker proudly carrying the Stars and Stripes.

During the afternoon, crowds packed St John's churchyard for another Thanksgiving Service which was preceded by a parade of over 700 young people representing the town's youth organisations who marched to the church from the South Street Car Park.

Once again the evening was turned over to dancing, but on this occasion, it was at the floodlit Huish Ground where a huge crowd danced to Bill Kelly's Band. There was a concert in the Sidney Gardens given by the Westland Male Voice Choir and the Salvation Army Band played in the Borough.

However, the highlight of the evening (quite literally) was the huge bonfire built on the top of Summerhouse Hill. At 10 o'clock precisely the bonfire was lit by Column Officer Charles Mitchell of the National Fire Service, and as the flames roared up they took with them a more than life-size effigy of Adolf Hitler whilst adults and children danced around the blaze.

During the following days across the nation, people danced, sang and thoroughly enjoyed themselves, forgetting, perhaps, for a short time, the savage war still to be fought to a conclusion in the Far East, and the shortages and rationing which would continue for a long time to come.

Yeovil got into party mood and all across the town children from toddlers to teenagers enjoyed tea and entertainment. Rationing was forgotten as the youngsters enjoyed the freely given food and soft drinks in quantities many had never previously experienced. In some streets, people brought out radios and gramophones, whilst others played accordions or pianos and concluding his day-long visit around the town to the many street parties the mayor exclaimed to a *Western Gazette* reporter that 'I've never seen so many happy faces in my life.'

Finally, the savage war in the Far East was brought to an end when the Japanese Empire surrendered on 14 August 1945 and at last, the world could celebrate the end on the Second World War which has broken out in 1939.

VJ-Day 15 August 1945

On Friday 17 August 1945, the *Western Gazette* reported that the announcement on midnight on Tuesday the 14th of the surrender of Japan:

'Caught the majority of people in the South and West unprepared for the immediate celebration of the end of the war. Comparatively few of the thousands of people who, for days, had so anxiously awaited the great news heard the Prime Minister Mr C. R. Attlee give the signal to all to "relax and enjoy themselves in the knowledge of work well done". Only in towns where social life is continued till a later hour was there immediate reaction to the relief which the announcement brought and quickly there were scenes of spontaneous rejoicing in the streets and in private houses. The majority of people were unaware of the return of peace until the first of the VJ-days was fairly well advanced. Then the preparations of local authorities and householders were accelerated and soon scenes reminiscent of VE-day were markedly in evidence. Throughout the South and West the celebrations were on much of the same scale and form as on the earlier occasion – thanksgiving services, ceremonial parades and music in the daytime, with the climax of fireworks, bonfires, the floodlighting of historic and public buildings, and dancing and unrestrained merrymaking in brilliantly lit streets and squares.

'Amid all the rejoicings there was grateful remembrance of the glorious part which the Hampshire, Dorset, Somerset and Wiltshire Regiments had played in the defeat of the enemy.'

Once again the *Gazette* caught the mood of the time in its report on the events of VJ-Day as they unfolded in Yeovil on that momentous occasion.

'Though there were remarkable scenes of joy and thanksgiving in Yeovil, there was no repetition of the wild hilarity which marked the end of the European war. Many workers who had not heard the radio announcements started out for work as usual. Townspeople were early astir, and hurriedly put out flags, bunting and streamers. Housewives formed long queues for food, but the longest queue was in Middle Street for fireworks.

'The Mayor and Corporation attended a thanksgiving service conducted by the Vicar of Yeovil (Preb. H. Mortlock Treen), at the parish church and the service was relayed to a gathering outside. The bells rang out their joyous peals throughout the day.

'Over 8,000 assembled in the Borough on Wednesday evening and were addressed by the Mayor (Mr W. S. Vosper), who asked them to remember with reverence and pride those who had fallen – both Servicemen and civilians – and those who had been maimed or wounded or were prisoners. He paid tribute to the work of the Forces and Civil Defence, and other services, and expressed the fervent hope that all would now be allowed to devote their thoughts and energies to the creation of a structure in which all people will live in real peace, happiness and prosperity.

'Public houses which had been granted an extension until midnight were forced to close their doors considerably earlier through lack of supplies. In some cases "Sold out" notices appeared before 10 o'clock.

'The Salvation Army gave a performance in Bide's Garden in the evening.

'Bill Kelly's Band provided music in the Borough, and there were boisterous scenes as the night wore on. Hundreds of people were singing, shouting and dancing. Floodlights blazed down until well after midnight and crackers, rockets and thunderflashes provided a constant succession of bangs and explosions. Two or three children had eye injuries – fortunately not serious – as a result of explosions. The beautiful old church stood floodlit in all its grandeur, and provided welcome solitude and peace only a few yards away from the dancing and singing crowds. There were also illuminations in Bide's Garden.

'An emergency centre manned by women members of the ladies' V.A.D. under Commandant Miss K. Marsh, at the Police Station dealt with a number of cases of fainting, and ambulances had several times to make their way through the crowd. Music came to an abrupt end at 11.40 when the wires from the microphone to the loudspeakers around the Borough were torn away but the crowd did not disperse until nearly three. An impromptu "band" played request items from the bandstand. A bonfire on the Mudford Road Playing Fields could be seen for miles around.'

All next day the bells of St John's church rang out and in the evening crowds again filled the Borough, singing and dancing till late, The pubs ran out of beer and cider and had to close early.

The town's children enjoyed parties during the days which followed, and once again out came the hoarded goodies to give them a time to remember.

18

FUN AT THE FÊTE

Looking back to the good times, perhaps village fêtes and jollifications could be some of the best of good times and so let us go back down memory lane.

Bishop's Lydeard

Fundraising to build a hut for the Bishop's Lydeard Boy Scouts' Troop was the theme of the scouts' fête in the Glebe Meadow on Thursday 24 May 1926.

The *Taunton Courier* reported that the event had attracted a large crowd and there high hopes of a 'useful sum of money being received'. The scoutmaster Commander G. O. R. Elliott, OBE, was in charge of the event and 'members of the Troop made themselves generally useful'. The Bishop Lydeard lads were helped by scout troops from Taunton's Huish School and Bagborough. The *Courier* went on to write that 'there were the usual amusements of the country fair', which included such delights as guessing competitions, a treasure hunt, 'walking the flower pots' and an 'aunt sally'. There was skittling for 'ladies and gentlemen' with a leg of lamb for the winner of the ladies' and a live pig was the gentleman's prize. No fête would be complete without the ice-cream and sweet stalls and it goes without saying that they were well patronised. Mr B. A. Christies' band from Bridgwater played popular music during the afternoon.

The Thursday evening featured exhibitions of folk dancing and scouts' first aid and signalling followed by a dance to the music of Mr Christies' band in the large marquee put up for the occasion on the Glebe Meadow.

Curry Rivel

Wednesday 21 July 1929, was the day of the Curry Rivel Church Organ Fund Fête in the 'beautiful grounds of Midelney Place, the home of Lieut-

Colonel Herring-Cooper. The threatening rain held off and the weather remained fine which was almost certainly why the *Taunton Courier* could report that the fête attracted a good attendance.

A marquee was set up on the lawn in front of the house for the stalls and sideshows. The stalls sold a variety of goods and vegetables, baskets, clothes and the ever-popular ice-creams and sweets and the sideshows included a coconut shy, a bran tub and a rather interesting parcel packing competition. There was a contest to 'name the baby' and another to win a live pig. 'Professor Burgess from Burnham the phrenologist' held consultations and Mrs and Miss Vincent told fortunes,

Outside there was a helter-skelter, tip-boat, children's pony rides and skittles. Pupils of Curry Rivel school performed folk and 'elf' dances whilst the Curry Rivel band played musical selections during the afternoon. Tea was served on the terrace of Midelney House with local ladies acting as waitresses dressed in Puritan costumes.

The day ended with evening dancing to the Curry Rivel band in the marquee.

Downside

According to the *Somerset Guardian and Radstock Observer,* ideal weather favoured the annual Downside Church Fête in the Vicarage grounds on Saturday afternoon 4 July 1953.

The sun shone and the children enjoyed the donkey rides whilst the grown-ups enjoyed the attractions of the stalls. There was one for skittles, another for croquet as well as stalls for the more esoteric sounding competitions of 'spinning jenny', 'clothes pegs', 'ring the bell', 'roll'em in', and 'doll in car' to name but a few. There were competitions for a pullover, cakes, buttonholes, fruit and cakes and all sorts of goodies.

One of the stalwarts of village fêtes, the children's fancy dress competition, was won by young Pat Church disguised as a 'Herald'.

Godney

The weather on Saturday 13 June 1953 was 'pleasant', just right for the Godney fête in Mr F. Church's field to raise funds for the village children's summer outing, the church and the village hall. The *Central Somerset Gazette* wrote that 'The event received the wholehearted support of the parishioners and it was most successful and enjoyable'.

Following the opening ceremony by Mr Eggington, the headmaster of Coxley Junior School, everyone got down the business of enjoying themselves. There were stalls and sideshows, competitions and sports for the children during the afternoon, followed by the adults in the early evening. One of the highlights of the evening was the tug-of-war which was won by Wells Young Farmers' Club. The day's proceedings ended with a dance in the village hall.

Horton

According to the *Taunton Courier* 'Fine weather favoured the Horton United Association Football Club fête held in the Recreation Ground on Saturday [16 August 1933] and 'a large crowd from the surrounding neighbourhood enjoyed an attractive programme of events.' On that fine Saturday afternoon, the fête was being held to raise funds for the Football and Hockey Club and the Nursing Association.

Two sporting events featured prominently in the programme, the first was a six-a-side football tournament for a challenge cup and medals. Ten teams took part and in the final Ilminster Hillsiders beat Horton 'B' to take the cup.

The second event was the final of the week-long village tennis tournament reported to have received a record number of entries. There were nine for the 'gents' singles', seven for the ladies' and seven for the ladies' doubles with 14 for the mixed. Mr Jeffries took the men's singles, Miss Scott from Chard the ladies' and the ladies' doubles was secured by Miss Hayball and Miss Baker; the mixed doubles were won by Miss Hayball and Mr Baker.

The Baby Show attracted a large entry in the three classes with Baby Capper winning the under 12 months, Baby Sheat the under ones and Baby Chard won the under twos.

The ever-popular 'ladies ankle' competition' was won by Mrs Harvey and her shapely ankle from nearby Broadway.

Stalls and sideshows did a brisk trade with the lucky-dip, hoop-la, quoits, bursting the balloon and 'topping the copper' being some of the most popular. The ice-cream stall did a roaring trade followed closely by the sweet stall.

During the afternoon and early evening, the Barrington Brass Band played selections on the Recreation Ground and the day was rounded off with a dance in the Victory Hall.

Pilton

The *Central Somerset Gazette* recorded on 14 August 1953 that 'Fine weather favoured the Fête and Flower Show arranged by the Pilton branch of the British Legion held in the attractive setting at the Manor House grounds (by kind permission of Lt.-Col. M.C.S. and Mrs Phipps on Saturday afternoon [8 August]. The Flower Show was one of the most successful ever staged in Pilton. Entries topped and surpassed those of last year by a big margin.'

Maypole dancing at a fête.

The show was held in a large marquee, where in addition to the colourful displays of flowers of every description there were competitions for vegetables, fruits, jams, and cakes as well as handicrafts with entries from adults and children. Outside on the lawns, there were sideshows, competitions, skittles, darts, a clock-golf and lots of other games of skill together with donkey rides for the children. During the late afternoon, there were family sports in a field next to the Manor House.

Upton

Whilst the Bible Christian Church Picnic was not a fête it seems that the participants had a thoroughly good time and which of course is one of the primary reasons for fêtes and other jollifications!

On 7 September 1907, the *West Somerset Free Press* wrote that Wednesday, 5 September was the day of the Upton Bible Christian Church's Picnic and visitors came to the venue at Upton Farm from a variety of different societies in all sorts of horse-drawn vehicles. They hailed from Bampton, Clayhanger, Raddington, Wiveliscombe, Huish Champflower, Clatworthy, Gupworthy, Dulverton and of course the village of Upton.

The visitors were all assembled by two o'clock and the picnic began with cricket and various other games. Two hours later over 150 sat down to a picnic meal given by 'Upton lady friends and nearly all the parishioners'.

During the evening a concert was given in the 'nicely decorated barn' at Upton Farm with an organ and piano loaned by Mr Purchase of Skilgate. Presiding at the concert was Mr Brown of the Upton Bible Christians who welcoming the visiting members of Baptist and Congregational chapels, Wesleyans, Church of England and Quakers, expressed his confidence that 'a social gathering of that sort mixed them up and did them all good', so wrote the *West Somerset Free Press* correspondent at the picnic. The concert began with a piano duet followed by a selection of songs both solos and duets, some recitations and concluded with an anthem from the Upton choir.

A coffee supper brought the picnic to an end, and tired but in good spirits. the visitors left for their homes in the variety of conveyances which had brought them.

Williton

The Williton Brotherhood held their second annual fête on Wednesday afternoon, 27 August 1912 on Mr Hosegood's field at the bottom of Long Street, and despite the threatening storm clouds the rain held off.

The chief feature of the fête was the sporting calendar with over 135 entries in the many events including flat races of varying distances, hurdles, and long and high jumps. In addition to the standard athletics, there were some slightly exotic events such as a 'Tortoise Bicycle race', a 'Ladies' Potato race' and a 'Wheelbarrow' race. One of the most popular events in the sporting calendar of many fêtes was the comic obstacle race which on this occasion included crawling through sacks, climbing ropes and getting over a horizontal beam at the top, eating a bun suspended on a string, jumping into a tub of water, then taking off wet socks and shoes and putting on dry ones and completing the race by fishing up the competitor's number from a tub of coloured water. There were two heats and a Mr F. Hawkins was the overall winner with the prize of a salad bowl for his efforts.

Two other competitions went down well with the visitors, one was the pillow fight in which the contestants sat astride a pole and tried to knock each other off with feather pillows. Williton's Mr H. Chilcott defeated all comers to win a watch. The second was skittles, with the first prize of a silver bicycle lamp. The alley was set up in a corner of the field and in addition to the first prize, the second was a jam dish, third a walking stick, number four a butter dish and a candlestick for the fifth.

Following all these activities, there was a high tea in a large marquee.

No fête would be complete without its sideshows and stalls and the Brotherhood's was no exception. There were coconut shies, hoop-las, a slide, swings and swing-boats, together with competitions of various sorts to name but a few, and stalls for sweets, fruit and vegetables and a multitude of goods of all descriptions.

Reporting on the event, the *West Somerset Free Press* wrote that one of the chief attractions was that of Mr Alfred Stenner's where:

'In a shed at the entrance to the field he had allowed to be exhibited a stuffed calf with two heads. The freak of nature came from Kimberley, South Africa having belonged to Mr Stenner's brother who brought it to England to be treated by a taxidermist. The animal lived for three months and was fed through both mouths.' The *Free Press* went on to reveal in its next edition on 31 August that Mr Stenner had put the 'phenomenon' up for sale.

During the afternoon, Mr Eli Barker's orchestra provided the musical entertainment and in the early evening the Minehead Male Voice Choir gave 'one of their delightful concerts to a large and appreciative crowd gathering round and listening with great pleasure to the programme, the pieces being unaccompanied'.

Sadly, the open-air evening dancing was brought to an abrupt end when the rain which had threatened all day finally decided to come down in great quantities.

Even so, it seemed that everyone had a good time.

19

THROUGH THE HEART OF SOMERSET

In the *Somerset Year Book* 1925 published by The Society of Somerset Folk, contributor H. Vicars Webb described a drive 'Through the Heart Of Somerset':

'A temperature equal to mid-June; a glorious sky and sunshine; a refreshing breeze to temper the warmth; superb scenes in cloudland; mile upon miles of golden meads; hundreds of acres of orchard land, radiant with apple blossom; hills and valleys smiling under brilliant light; birdlife at its greatest activity, and the air full of song; all this and much more, was experienced in a motor run from Bristol down to the Quantock country.

'The forward route was taken through Long Ashton, Flax Bourton, West Town, and Cleeve to Congresbury. Then on to Churchill, beautiful in its setting of Maytime glory, where a brief stop was made. On again through Rowberrow and the charming vale of Winscombe, and up the ascent to Shute Shelve Hill where slopes are aflame with gorse. Down the steep descent to the village of Cross, and away through the rich pastures dominated by Crook's Peak and Wavering Down. On the overhead wires, one is glad to see at frequent intervals, swallows resting after their long pursuit of insect prey. a sparrow hawk suddenly appears and crosses the roadway, low down, so that its barred under-plumage can be readily noted.

"Brent Knoll is passed, and a few minutes later we cross the Brue at Highbridge, and slip away through Dunball, on the banks of the Parrett, to Bridgwater, the birthplace of the renowned Admiral Blake. Another brief halt here to renew associations with boyhood days. On leaving, we take the road to Nether Stowey, and press on, having the undulating contour of the Quantocks in full view. The village of Stowey ever remains memorable for its associations with the immortal Coleridge and of Thomas Poole and his friends. Situated close to the church, and attached to the Court, we note that quaint structure, known as the Gazebo, said to have been a look-out apartment for the passing of the old Minehead coach. The poet's cottage is soon passed. The lovely hills skirt the roadway at Doddington, and from this point we quickly reach our destination.

Brent Knoll.

'It is Springtime in Holford Glen. The music and magic of May is at its height on the glorious hills, and in their beauteous combes. Many of Holford's charms are hidden away and must be sought for. Nature is here lavish with her gifts, and even seeks to veil from our eyes secrets of beauty. Some of the waterfalls, giving out their musical cadences, can scarcely be seen, so dense is the green verdure. For the nature lover these combes and hills and woods are shrines, and as such must ever remain.

'Our homeward journey was only slightly changed. From Highbridge we diverted to the Burnham sea front, and enjoyed the evening breeze, as the sky was preparing for a grand effect. This developed as we proceeded, and the sunset of a perfect day was one of supreme grandeur.'

20

THE 'WAYZGOOSE'

A LITTLE WHILE AGO your author was looking through the columns of *Pulman's Weekly News* when he came across the headline 'Our Annual Wayzgoose', and reading on discovered that the article in question was a report on an outing enjoyed by the staff of *Pulman's Weekly News* and its sister paper, the *Western Gazette*. Looking, where else but to the Internet, he found that a 'Wayzgoose' was the name given to the annual excursion or dinner of the staff of a printing works or newspaper. It seems that the annual event evolved from the traditional entertainment given by a master printer to his workmen each year to celebrated St Bartholomew's Day on 24 August, which marked the traditional end of summer and working by candlelight began.

To continue, on Saturday 8 July 1899, the newspapers' annual Wayzgoose was to London on a special excursion train put on by the London and South Western Railway Company, and *Pulman's* wrote that 'according to custom, the staff gave the public the opportunity of sharing the advantages of the organised trip and the result was that nearly 900, in addition to about a 100 members of the staff left Yeovil for a long day out in Town'.

Many of the excursionists had an early morning trip into Yeovil from Crewkerne, Martock, Stoke and surrounding villages to leave with the main party from Yeovil Town Station at 5.15 am, prompt. The long train pulled by two locomotives, made brief stops at Yeovil Junction and Sherborne to pick up more passengers, and arrived at Waterloo Station just after nine o'clock.

Leaving the excursionists to enjoy the attractions of the capital, including a Grand Review of Volunteer Regiments in St James's Park and the London Zoo, the staff made their way to Earl's Court Exhibition Centre where, after assembling in the Western Gardens, they were entertained by the directors of the newspapers' parent company to an excellent hot luncheon provided by Messrs Spierce and Pond in the Chop House.

The meal, presided over by the chairman of the company, The Rt. Hon, Lord Montagu of Beaulieu, was followed by a toast proposed by the editor, Mr G. F. Munford, to the Proprietors, thanking them for their generous hospitality and the interest taken in the welfare of their employees.

Lord Montagu responded as did the managing director, Mr Trevor Davies, and the proceedings concluded with a toast to Her Majesty the Queen and the singing of the National Anthem.

There was no set programme for the rest of the day, some of the staff left for central London whilst others remained to enjoy the attractions in the Centre's grounds and the Great Britain Exhibition 1899, the Great Wheel and 'a hundred and one side shows'.

After a long day, the journey back to Yeovil left Waterloo Station at 12.20 a.m., reaching home at half-past four in the morning 'all unanimously of the opinion that the trip had been one of the most pleasant ever held'.

The annual Wayzgoose of the staff of the *Somerset Herald* and *Taunton Courier* was held on Sunday14 July 1890 when at 8 o'clock a party of 25 left Taunton Railway Station and travelled to Minehead where a 'well-appointed four horse char-a-banc and other carriages awaited them'. Following 'an excellent drive' along the Porlock road they arrived at the residence of Sir Thomas Acland at Holnicote 'and rambled up a leafy lane, prettily embowered in trees' to Selworthy Green surrounded by 'the old-fashioned cottages known as Selworthy almshouses'. On to Selworthy church to explore the interior and climb up the tower to the fine views of Exmoor and Dunkery Beacon. Leaving the church the party rambled down to the pretty village of Bossington where they rejoined their conveyances and travelled on to Porlock Weir for dinner provided 'by host Godard' at the Anchor Hotel. Following dinner there were speeches and toasts, after which suitably refreshed the party split, one to enjoy 'an agreeable yachting trip in the bay' and the other walked over the steep path to the tiny Culbone church.

Returning to Porlock Weir tea was taken at the Anchor after which the party was driven to Minehead where they spent 'a pleasant couple of hours' and returned home the Taunton on the last train.

Reporting on the Wayzgoose the *Taunton Courier* wrote that 'The Excursionists were favoured with excellent weather throughout the day, and it was generally agreed that the outing was one of the most pleasant that the staff has ever had.'

The Esplanade showing Bungalow Tea Rooms, Minehead.

21

'WURTS, LOOKING AT A FIELD OF WHEAT AND AN OLD YELLOW WAGGON'

SOMERSET AUTHOR, YEOVIL-BORN Walter Raymond (1852-1931), wrote popular books and articles for over 30 years, but today, sadly, he is almost forgotten, even in his beloved Somerset and the town of his birth.

For sixteen years, Walter Raymond rented a cottage in Withypool, which he named 'Hazelgrove-Plucknut' in the many articles he wrote about the Exmoor village for national newspapers and periodicals and in the two much-loved books published in the early years of the last century – *The Book of Simple Delights* and *The Book of Crafts and Character.*

The following extracts from *The Book of Simple Delights,* first published in 1906 and which ran for at least four editions, describes the gathering of whortleberries or 'wurts' on the moor above the village, looking at a field of wheat on hot summer's day and a ride on an old yellow waggon.

'Wurts'

The village children have just started their summer holidays and with three youngsters the author sets out to harvest some 'wurts'.

'For the whortleberries – "wurts" they called them, and even "hurts' – were turning purple-ripe on the moor, and the holidays had begun. Those summer holidays, that began on no fixed date, but were a removable festival, changing according to the season, so that the children might gather the wild harvest of the moorland. There were little more than a score though they made enough noise for a hundred as they ran down the village street.

'I have an affection for this moorland village street. It is so far away, so quaint so old world.

'It runs along the hill-side, with little by-ways up the incline, so that the houses stand one behind and above the other. But the squat embattle tower of the old grey church rears higher than them all.

'Before each cottage is a slanting garden. Ranks of peas and tall scarlet runners, laden at the time with flowers, as well as files of broad beans with black bulging pods left too long without picking, run parallel with the path of flat stones from the front door to the hatch. There are tall hollyhocks, groups of blue monks-hood, and here and there a fuchsia bush, bearing tiny red flowers less than an inch in length.

'All sorts of creepers clamber over the white-washed fronts and geraniums blind the downstair windows. There is a clothes-line, too, from which, when the air is drying, household clouts and wonderful garments of many hues and sizes flutter gaily in the wind. The faggot pile and dark brown stack of turves stand close by. The smoke that rises out of the chimneys is blue and has no smuts.

'Down the valley, merrily humming around rocks and boulders, leaps the silver river; and above the woods and the enclosed fields that skirt its course, both before and behind the village, lies the broad moor where the whortleberries grow.

'It is quite a little industry, this picking of "wurts," though it lasts only about three weeks. No other fruit possesses so unexpected a flavour. None gives so fine a blend of with the scald-cream, which is one of the most admirable institutions of the neighbourhood. So there is invariably a great demand. And when the crop is small, why, the price goes so much higher. We must all go "a-wurting." If not for trade, as a sort of picnic.

'To Norton Moor we went.

'We began with a mile of lane. But a glorious lane between walled banks with sheltering beech hedgerows high above. On either hand were bright green ferns and tall purple foxgloves, to which great bumble-bees paid visits, buzzing from flower to flower all up the tapering stem, and silent only when they crept in to drink. Wild strawberries, with deep crimson fruit, sprang from the crevices and hung ripening above the mossy stones. Wild raspberries, too, on Lilliputian canes, drawing an ancestry, it may be, from bird-carried seed of a more cultured stock, flourished in profusion.'

'Out of the shady lane, by a narrow pathway up the slope, where bracken grows waist-high after the old heather has been burnt off, we climbed to the ridge of the open breezy moor. Masses of purple heather and the paler-coloured ling were in full flower: and growing amongst them, and intermingled everywhere, was the little dark green myrtle-shaped leaf, that half conceals a berry almost the size of a black-currant and covered with a thicker bloom than the wild sloe. Honey-bees were humming on all sides, and butterflies went flitting by in the sun. Upon the brown hillside of the next ridge, where wild ponies were dotted about and here and there broke the even line against the sky, was passing the dark shadow of an August thundercloud.'

'Of Looking at a Field of Wheat'

'In the still air my wheat-field was as tranquil as an inland lake. Not a ripple disturbed its surface. The ears bent over one towards the other under the burning heat as if asleep. Some of them, that held their heads an inch or two above their fellows, looked as if they were painted on the pale grey of the horizon. Even the taller wild oat sprinkled here and there throughout the crop, so slight and graceful that it shivered at the merest breath, was still. It had nothing more in the world to do but to stand in the sun, ripen and shed its seed. Even then the oat hung loosely in the open husk, ready to fall before harvest, and lie securely on the ground. There need be no anxiety. The future crop of wild oats will not fail.

'I pushed my way along the hedgerow on the narrow strip of rough herbage between the ditch and the standing corn. Here the crop was thin when rabbits feed in the spring. Honeysuckles climbed and wild roses sprawled all over the hedge, mingling with the white, bell-shaped flowers of the woodbine and the broad shining leaves of the black bryony, that becomes paler and smaller the further the plant pushes its way.

'There came a sweet-brier scent from the hedge roses, this hot noonday of late summer, after the rain, though there was little song from the birds. They had hatched their last broods. The countryside was full of their progeny, and for the most part they had ceased to sing. Yet you might sometimes hear the skylark, that built its nest in April between the drills when this same field of wheat was green. And the robin, who keeps a merry heart all year through. And though they were mute that day, the sparrows that chatter so loudly around the village eaves in company with various of their cousins, the finches, flew across the path from the corn to the shelter of the hedgerow in such increasing swarms that the music of their wings was like the continual humming over a mill-wheel. They had made the corn scanty close to the hedge. The ground below was thickly bestrewn with the chaff they had thrown down getting at the grain. In front of me I could see them fluttering close to the ear, for the slender stems.

'Near to the oak the ditch was dry and here I contrived what my landlord so quaintly called a "bushment" by pulling down the leafy boughs to form a bower.

'My bower had a garden in front and beyond that lay the untrodden forest of wheat. The field convolvulus had twined around the nearest corn as if to throttle them, its delicately veined flowers wide open to the light; and the tiny pimpernel, the "shepherd's weather-glass," looked up from the ground, its little red petals turned back until they were flat because the day was bright. There were smaller scarlet poppies on their hairy stems, yellow marigolds and blue cornflowers with stalks so slender yet so tough that reapers long ago gave them the name of "blunt sickles." There were purple cockles, as by the gate, tall and erect, as if in scorn of the pale little

Withypool.

heartsease at their feet. And the air was filled with the scent of wild mint that had been trodden under my feet and crushed as I was making the bushment.

'All living things of the cornfield came quite close to me without suspicion of my presence. Sometimes there came a rustle amongst the standing corn and the ears shook, although there was no wind. That was a hare travelling along her run, a beaten track amongst the straight stems of the upright corn, smooth as a well-used path through a forest of pines. A rabbit crossed from the wheat to the hedgerow, and presently a stoat on the same track.

'Towards afternoon there came a low cluck from the other side of the hedge. Presently, close to the oak tree, a covey of partridge came through a gap that had been stopped with a hurdle. They stayed awhile and dusted themselves on the dry bank under the shady branches. They were close enough to be counted, and all the little, unconscious workings of their minds could be observed.

'To watch them was a real delight.'

'An Old Yellow Waggon'

'My landlord has a very old yellow waggon. I saw it first in his hayfield, but then its graceful lines were hidden underneath the overhanging load. But on the day when the last sheaf was hauled in my field of wheat, it was left beside the stack. The horses stood at rest under the cool shelter of the hedgerow. The men were sitting near on a bank with their bits of lunch. There was a jar also from which to drink "good luck" all round. For this is as much as remains to-day of the old feast of "Harvest Home."

'I went and looked at the old waggon more closely. It had been patched and mended many a time, and perhaps little or nothing of the original fabric remained. It had already lived more than half a century and was serviceable still.

'If that old yellow waggon could have spoken, he would have told me of many changes. He – we call everything "he", even to the old cow looking over the hedgerow – he was built by the village wainwright. The name may still be read upon the tail-board, and found again upon a leaning headstone in the village churchyard.

'The modern waggon is often the offspring of a city waggon-works more than fifty miles away. It is honest work, no doubt, at a fair price. But it can no more compare with the other, than the houses of to-day can rival the architecture of the past.

'This old waggon, in spite of his years, still possesses personal beauty and an air of distinction. Look at the graceful curves of his lades, those flat projecting rails along its sides, upon which the youth and beauty of past generations have ridden to picnics in comfort and without loss of dignity. And in his young days the waggon really brought the harvest home. When the golden stacks or mows were built in the mow-barton close to the homestead and handy to the "barn's door." How rich and how bright they looked against the older thatch! The introduction of machinery for threshing has brought about this change. Now it saves labour to built the mow where the crop was grown. The engine drags the thresher out into the field, and very soon after harvest its musical humming note may be heard all around, the countryside. Yet folk can remember when the old waggon was new, and when men threshed with "drashles" on the barn's floor, will tell you that there has never been prettier music than the thump, thump of two flails with a cuckoo calling in between.

'Machinery has driven away many another old-world custom.

'The chains jingled, the horses were shoved in place and harnessed to depart.

'"You'll be pleased to ride?" said the carter.

'So I climbed up and sat upon the raves, and we all rode home together, creaking and jolting over the ruts of the lane. But my soul was moved to pity for that poor old waggon, and my heart nearly leapt into my mouth at every yard we went. He groaned and seemed to twist and writhe as if it were an agony to travel. Alas! No oils can ever again lubricate those creaking old joints of his into ease.

'It was otherwise in his gallant youth, when he carried home the "Harvest Queen."

'She was a figure made of a gigantic sheaf, and clad in the brightest garments the village could produce. Her head was crowned with flowers. Under her arm she carried another sheaf, and in one hand a "reap hook." She was covered in garlands, and set upon the last load, which also was festooned with flowers. And every living soul who had lent a hand at the harvest on that farm ran by the side and shouted and sang. And so they brought the last load home to the mow-barton and the "barn's door."

'There was a supper in the homestead kitchen, or in the barn, that night – a great rump of beef and a plum pudding half as large as a bushel basket, with a sauce of laughter, goodwill, and song – and a fiddler made one of the company.

'There was a deal of spilling and drinking "two" in those days; but the mirth was wholesome and promoted good feeling and did no harm to anybody.

'We have lost the hearty old customs, but what has the young villager found in place of them?

'A cheap excursion now and then to the seaside or even some distant city is a poor compensation for the circle of feasts and pastimes now almost forgotten which formerly enlivened the rural year.'

The *Western Gazette* in its obituary to Walter Raymond on 10 April 1931, wrote that he was; 'A national writer who wrote about Somerset because he knew and loved the county. He made his readers feel and see the places and people they loved so well. He has been described as the "Thomas Hardy of Somerset."

22

YEOVIL SHOW'S CENTENARY

On a Friday evening in early September 1833, the Portreeve of Yeovil, Robert Jennings, took the Chair at a public meeting in the Mermaid Inn when it was agreed to hold an Annual Cattle Show at the town's Christmas Great Market. The Show would be organised by a Society under the Chairmanship of J. Phelips Esq. with John Batten Esq. as Honorary Secretary, and competition for the first event at the 1833 Christmas Great Market was so intense that extra prizes had to be given.

One hundred years later, the Yeovil Agricultural Society held its Centenary Show at the new site at Barwick Park on Thursday 14 September 1933, and during this time it had grown from a local cattle show to one of the largest one-day agricultural events in the country.

Earlier Shows had been held at several venues, including fields under Babylon Hill over the River Yeo in Dorset. In 1932 the great Bath and West Show had been a success at Barwick Park and the Agricultural Society decided to relocate the 1933 Centenary Show to this spacious new site. The exhibition area extended over 30 acres laid out with a broad avenue leading to the main ring, flanked on the right by areas for cattle, sheep, goats and pigs, whilst on the left were the machinery and trade exhibitions and the huge poultry marquee; at the south of the ground were the horses and ponies together with the horticultural tent. The new site also provided much-improved traffic access and parking for over 1000 cars.

Show day opened in brilliant sunshine and from the start, there was a continuous stream of people and cars to the ground. The Show competitions included sections for cattle, sheep, goats, pigs, agricultural horses, hunters, ponies, poultry, rabbits, cheese, butter, clotted cream, cider, honey, fruit, vegetables and floral displays. Competition had always been keen and more so at the Centenary Show with the Prince of Wales' challenge trophy to be won outright for the best dairy cow of any breed and open to exhibitors from within a radius of 30 miles of Yeovil who had not won a prize for cattle during the previous five years at any exhibition held for two or more consecutive days. Farmer Hugh Francis of Templecombe's dairy cow was the winner. The Prince also entered a Devon dairy cow called 'Climsland Gay Lassie' from one of the Duchy of Cornwall farms but it failed to win a prize.

The Poultry Show continued to maintain its reputation as one of the largest and best in the country, attracting competitors from as far away as the North of England and Scotland. The *Western Gazette* believed that the poultry marquee was the only one in the country to be lit by electric light.

Yeovil Showground.

At the popular Trades Fair there were displays and exhibitions ranging from radios, pianos, printers and sports gear to seedsmen and agricultural engineers.

The main non-agricultural feature was a Royal Naval field gun display and competition in the main ring between a team of seamen and one of stokers. The teams began by changing the wheels from the gun to the limber, two rounds were fired, the guns limbered up and the wheels changed back. The stokers won by a close margin – the operations, in the words of the *Western Gazette's* reporter 'being carried out with machine-like precision.' In the display which followed, the guns were brought into action, fired, pulled around the ring, fired again, dismantled, each gun barrel lashed to the limber and trotted out of the ring – all drills being controlled by whistles.

Between 12,000 and 15,000 people attended the Show from all across Somerset and the neighbouring counties and many of whom no doubt refreshed themselves in the hospitality tents including the *Western Gazette's* 'rest tent'.

23

THE BOYS' BRIGADE CAMP – 1906

THE AFTERNOON OF Saturday 23 June 1906, saw the 120 strong Yeovil and District Battalion of the Boys' Brigade arrive at Blue Anchor Station, disembark, form up in ranks and march the short distance to the field adjoining the railway station for their week's annual camp. The camp was laid out in true military style with three lines of tents to accommodate the lads of the 1st and 2nd Yeovil companies, together with companies from Bridgwater, Dorchester, Ilminster, Milborne Port and Stoke-sub-Hamdon. Meals would be served in a large marquee, which would also act as the venue for the camp concert, there was a canteen 'where aerated waters, fruit &c. are obtainable', an officers' mess, a hospital tent and 'the water supply

The Boys' Brigade Camp at Blue Anchor.

and sanitary arrangements are excellent'. No sooner had the boys settled in when a violent thunderstorm rolled over the camp and 'where to counteract any feeling of depression', the battalion assembled in the marquee. To the crash of thunder, the lads sang sacred songs until the storm went on its way and they returned to their surprisingly dry tents.

A bugle sounded reveille at six o'clock on Sunday morning (as it would for the rest of the week), there were two services and during the evening there was a 'drumhead muster' attended by several hundred 'visitors', and accompanied by the battalion's drum and bugle band. Lights out at ten o'clock ended the first full day.

Apart from Tuesday and Friday, the days were taken up with drills, sports of various kinds and sea bathing 'under strict supervision, a local boat being in attendance and a bugle gives the signal for entering and leaving the water'.

Early on Tuesday morning the battalion left camp in high spirits and took the train to Minehead where they boarded one of Messrs P & A Campbell's paddle steamers and sailed (free of charge) on a day trip to Ilfracombe. The Channel was calm and it seems that no one succumbed to sea-sickness.

Thursday afternoon's sports were called off due to weather, and despite the rain, the evening camp concert in the large marquee was 'bright and joyful', one of the contributors being the Carhampton Mouthorgan Band.

On Friday the battalion travelled to Dunster where they were inspected 'on the bowling green by Captain A.F. Luttrell, M.P. and entertained to tea'.

The camp broke up on Saturday morning and the battalion took the train back to Taunton where the companies went their several ways home; for many of the lads this was the only holiday they would have in 1906 and for some, it would have been the first-ever.

Following the departure of the Yeovil and District Battalion, the local *West Somerset Free Press* commented; 'A word should be said in praise of the conduct of the lads, which has been exemplary throughout, and they on their part have been charmed, apart from the unpleasant weather, with what is their first, but they hope will by no means be their last visit, to West Somerset.

24

THE FORESTERS' FÊTE

Tuesday 1 August 1866, was the day of the Ancient Order of Foresters' Fête. Members of the Court 'Yeovil's Pride' were somewhat down-hearted by the light rain which fell in the early morning, but by mid-day, the breeze had blown the dark clouds away, and spirits were high again.

People poured into Yeovil by the hundreds, many coming by train on cheap excursions run by the Bristol and Exeter Railway Company, and the other lines serving the town. Foresters from Courts at Sherborne, Taunton, Bridgwater and elsewhere in the area, assembled at the Hendford Station Yard where a procession was formed and led by 'Yeovil's Pride' the Foresters set out to march through the streets to Newton Park where food and entertainment awaited.

The brethren of the order, wearing their full regalia and carrying banners, flags and emblems, were followed by the Mayor, Alderman Edward Raymond, in his carriage and a wagon containing the Taunton 'Maypole Dancers'. Other personages to be seen in the parade were, 'Miniature Robin Hood' on horseback, Friar Tuck, another wagon in which a lounging Robin Hood was taking his last bow shot before he expired and a conveyance with a shepherd, shepherdess and sheep on board. Music accompanying the marchers was provided by the bands of the 16th and 21st Companies of the Somerset Rifle Volunteers.

Arriving at Newton Park, the brethren sat down in a large marquee to an excellent dinner provided by Mr Slade of the Full Moon, and presided over by the Mayor, 'supported by several gentlemen of the town and neighbourhood'.

During the afternoon, a large number of people visited the Park, where a variety of amusements had been provided. There was archery, football, donkey racing, Aunt Sally, Uncle Sam, bowling and Maypole Dancing. Sergeant Dominy, of the Queen's Own Dorset Yeomanry, performed

Newton Woods and Park.

breathtaking (if not potentially fatal) feats of skill with his sword, which involved placing an apple on a silk handkerchief and severing it without injuring the handkerchief and slicing apples, gooseberries, potatoes and eggs placed on a very brave boy's hand and head without injuring the lad. The sergeant also severed a sheep and two bars of lead with a single stroke. All this excitement was accompanied by the bands of the Volunteers. A cold luncheon could be bought from Mr Slade for two shillings in his refreshment tent, a shilling tea at Mr Tomkins' marquee and Mr Brooke did a brisk trade from his confectionary stall.

During the evening there was dancing in the large marquee and so ended what was reported to have been a very successful Fête.

However, some people never seem satisfied, and the following letter from LOOKER ON appeared in the following week's *Yeovil Times*:

'Sir, In your edition of yesterday you were rather too lenient when you say "The Foresters' Fête on Tuesday passed off very successfully, and members of the Court 'Yeovil's Pride' may well be congratulated thereon." At least the fête was not a complete success, nor was it so successful as it might have been. Of course the committee were anxious to clear as much as they could, but it appeared to me that they went a little too far in that direction. A large number of persons in the field complained that the bands were prevented from playing dancing tunes during the afternoon, except a simple polka for the May-pole dancers. In the evening complaints were even more numerous, as the Yeovil Band was positively stopped when it had commenced playing. Many persons objected to going into the tent where the dancing was carried on, and which was the only place where a dance could be indulged in, as the musicians were only allowed to play dance music beneath the canvas. Others objected to the extra shilling which was charged for admission to the tent, which they considered exorbitant. Two shillings, *perhaps* was not too much for a cold dinner, but the tea would probably have been more successful had the charge been rather lower. Some of those who had been employed by the managers of the affair, too, complained loudly in the field that agreements were not faithfully carried out, and that neither refreshments not money was forthcoming as readily as they ought to have been.'

25

CLEVEDON'S BANK HOLIDAY AND FLOWER SHOW 1910

According to the *Weston-super-Mare Gazette* of 6 August 1911, August Bank Holiday Monday on the first day of the month there was a 'Big influx of visitors to Clevedon, and went on to report that:

'Old Clevedonians – and they are legion – assert that it is many, many years since such a large concourse of visitors came to Clevedon, as on Bank Holiday. And we can quite believe it, for the place was simply packed on Monday, and with the fine weather during the greater portion of the day, the holiday at Clevedon was one round of happy success.

'A pleasing feature of the day's proceedings was the orderly behaviour of the huge crowd of holiday-makers and trippers. In fact, seldom has the day passed so quietly as regards the conduct of visitors. With the fine array of bright and seasonable dresses worn by the ladies, and the gaily attired juveniles, the Sea Front was literally lined, and other favourite places of resort were also well patronised. It is interesting to note that a big influx of persons came from London and other large places came to Clevedon for the weekend so that with the many day-trippers, the total number of visitors was probably in excess of the resident population.

'In addition to those who came by boat and train, the traffic on the road was exceptionally heavy whilst there were many who used motors, and a good many more used the bicycle as a means of locomotion. There was a big increase in the number of horse vehicles used. In fact, no less than twenty-seven horse brakes and waggonettes passed through East Clevedon in the space of a couple of hours or so.

'With the tide serving well, boating was largely indulged in, the motor boat being a special favourite. The pier had been decorated, and the Promenade Band played all day to some large audiences. Capital concerts were given on the Green beach by those good artistes, "The Concerts", whilst the Salvation Army Band from Midsomer Norton provided some delightful music in the Triangle and on the Beach.

'There were the usual children's sports on the sands and the youngsters seemed to have had a very happy time, whilst the various walking places were well patronised. Taken altogether, the holiday proved an enjoyable one, and remarkably pleasant, the extra police drafted into the town having little occasion to interfere with the visitors.'

One of the highlights of the Bank Holiday time at Clevedon was the Clevedon Horticultural Society's Flower Show held on Tuesday and Wednesday 2 and 3 August 1910, in a field off Victoria Road.

Clevedon.

The *Weston-super-Mare Gazette* reported that despite the rain which had begun on Monday night and which had, without doubt, resulted in the lower attendance, the two-day show had proved a success. There was a record of 600 entries in all classes compared with 400 in 1909 and in the judges' opinion the quality of the produce 'much much above the average for a show like the Clevedon one'. The *Gazette* went on to report that on Tuesday the 'show proper took place and was followed by the athletic sports and distribution of show prizes'.

The Clevedon Horticultural Society was formed in 1869 and held its first show later that year. It was a great success from the start and apart from the duration of the two World Wars (1914-18 and 1939-45) and its postponement in 2020 due to the corona virus pandemic, the show has run continuously since its foundation. During these years the show has been held at a number of venues in Clevedon finally settling in the Salthouse Fields in the late 1960s.

26

A 'RESPECTABLY ESTABLISHED' CRICKET CLUB

From the *Taunton Courier* of Wednesday 15 July 1829:

'CRICKET.-It is with great satisfaction we observe the spirit which seems to be infused in the Club, recently formed in this town [Taunton], for the purpose of playing that manly and recreative game; and although most of the players have just but entered on the practice of the amusement, yet the progress already made seems to bid fair for its becoming a constant source of gratification. It has been long remarked that this town possesses no kind of sportive institution for young men, and we therefore rejoice in the successful formation of the Cricket Club, which has been recently and respectably established, and cordially wish for its permanence and prosperity.'

The writer's wish was granted, the Club became 'respectably established', and nine years later on Wednesday 1 August 1838, the *Taunton Courier* could record that:

'The Cricket-match between the Taunton and Sidmouth Clubs, took place yesterday, at Orchard Portman, near this town. Much skill at batting was exhibited on both sides, and many fine runs ensued, but the Tauntonians had by the far best of it, and the match was decided accordingly. Several carriages, graced with female beauty and attractiveness, were on the ground, which was in excellent order for the sport. Upwards of 200 gentlemen sat down to a very superior dinner (supplied by Mr Durk, of Shoreditch Inn), in a large marquee in the field, and every thing passed off with *ecláte*, amidst the most friendly rivalry. The whole scene on this occasion was singularly brilliant, and we were glad to hear a just meed* of compliment paid to the active Secretary of the Club (Mr Eales White), for the complete success of his very judicious arrangements. The play was highly interesting. The whole of "The Taunton Men" employed every nerve, with admirable steadiness; this, with the bowling of Mr Rich, the neat catches of Messrs. West and Coles, the wicket-keeping of Mr Gillam, the "long-stop" of Mr C. Sweet, together with the extraordinary play of Mr Pole (who made 59 off his bat in one inning), appeared too much for the Sidmouth eleven; the latter making 66 runs in both innings, the Taunton 137 *in one inning!* Nothing could exceed the kindness and good feeling mutually evinced on the occasion. We were glad to see that none but absolute members of each Club were in either "eleven," and, more so, that nothing, occurred to disturb the general harmony. The Taunton go to Sidmouth on the 22nd, to play the return match. Edwards Beadon, Esq. and Captain Maher ably officiate as President and Vice President at the Dinner.'

From the *Taunton Courier* of Wednesday 29 August 1838:

'TAUNTON AND SIDMOUTH CRICKET CLUBS. – The return match was played at Sidmouth on Friday last. Taunton first took the bat, and made 54 runs. Sidmouth then defended the wickets from the artillery of Messrs. Rich, and counted 28. Taunton second innings scored 98, and Sidmouth, for the first four bats, 19, when "night, put an end to the combat," Sidmouth having 7 wickets to go down. The weather on the following

Sidmouth Cricket Field.

morning proved a damper to any desire for renewing the contest; thus Taunton may fairly claim the advantage, being 114 majority at the close of play. The ground was graced by a galaxy of beauty and fashion, and crowded with persons evincing considerable interest in the progress of the game. The weather was singularly beautiful, and the breezes from the adjoining ocean, were wafted in refreshing zephyrs to the thronged scene of contention. Nothing could exceed the polite and hospitable attentions of the occasion: a spacious tent was provided for the ladies, under which was provided an abundance of fruit, wines and other delicacies, whilst a sumptuous dinner awaited the combatants and their friends in the room, the contiguity of which the town offered the unusual assistance to the "commissariate department," which was most generously taken advantage of at this time. The best feeling was interchanged, and a hope, universally expressed, to meet again next season. The very agreeable day terminated by an exchange of *bats* for *pumps* at a very numerously attended ball'.

*meed = Old

27

QUEEN VICTORIA'S DIAMOND JUBILEE

On 20 June 1837, eighteen-years-old Victoria became Queen of the United Kingdom of Great Britain and Ireland, and when sixty years later she celebrated her Diamond Jubilee on Tuesday 22 June 1897, the United Kingdom was 'top nation' with the largest Empire the world had ever seen.

Across Somerset, Jubilee Day dawned cloudy and dull with a hint of rain in the air, but as the morning wore on, the sun broke through to provide, in the words of the *Western Gazette* a day of 'real Queen's weather'. However, the Volunteers' Band got up early and accompanied a number of friends in rendering 'God Save the Queen' and other patriotic songs during the early hours of Jubilee day outside St John's church.

Just after 5 o'clock, the Yeovil blacksmiths were up and about indulging in the joys of making loud bangs by placing small explosive charges on their anvils and hitting them with hammers, and when the bells of St John's parish church began to ring out across the town, anyone hoping for a lie-in (the day had been declared a holiday) would be sorely disappointed!

The fronts of the town's shops, pubs, houses and public buildings were covered in a wide variety of decorations and the Borough was described as a 'perfect kaleidoscope of banners, streamers and bunting arranged in rich and tasteful profusion'. Even the workhouse in Preston Road was reported to be 'superbly decorated'. All this in honour, to quote the *Gazette*, of 'The Queenliest of Queenly women'.

At 10 o'clock, F Company of the Somerset Light Infantry Rifle Volunteers paraded in the Borough and fired off a 'feu-de-joi', the Volunteers' Band played the National Anthem and they all marched to St John's churchyard where they joined some 2000 people assembled for the open-air commemoration service.

A 'Public Luncheon' was held at Wyndham Field at 1 o'clock, but compared with the Golden Jubilee luncheon of June 1887 when several thousand sat down to eat, this year's was poorly supported despite 'the catering leaving nothing to be desired' and much to the disappointment of the organizers.

The highlight of the day took place at half-past two when the park now known as Sidney Gardens was presented to the town. It was the gift of the Mayor, Alderman Sidney Watts, but as he was in London representing the town at the Jubilee Celebrations in the capital, the ceremony was carried out by his two daughters Ada and Mildred. The *Western Gazette* estimated that over 5000 people, including at least 3500 Sunday School children and their teachers witnessed the ceremony as Ada handed the deeds of the land to the Deputy Mayor, Alderman William Cox. The newspaper reported that she then planted a memorial tree declaring 'it to be well and truly planted in Sidney Gardens and hope that it will grow and flourish and thus hand down to future generations the story of the ever-to-be-reminded 22nd day of June 1897 – God Save the Queen!' The deputy mayor gave a speech of thanks and presented Ada with a solid gold chain as a memento of the occasion, Miss Bertha Davis handed her a bouquet of 'choice flowers', three cheers were given and 'For he's a jolly good fellow' sung.

Now came the part of the celebrations for which almost certainly, most of the 3500 children were looking forward to – the procession to Wyndham Field for the Children's Tea and Sports.

The procession formed up and set off with the Military Band in the lead, followed by the deputy mayor, members of the town council and officials (all in carriages) and on foot the Jubilee Committee, Volunteer Fire Brigade, 'Gentlemen and Tradesmen of the Town', Friendly Societies with banners aloft, the Town Band, the children waving their flags and banners and the Salvation Army Band. Watched by a large crowd the procession wound its way along Preston Road, down through Kingston to Princes Street, through High Street across the Borough into Middle Street to Wyndham Field for tea and sports at four o'clock.

At five o'clock prompt it was time for nearly 500 'old folks' to sit down and enjoy the 'meat tea for Old People upwards of 60 years of age in a marquee'.

Newton Park was the venue for the more serious Adult Sports at half-past five and here a large crowd watched a variety of cycle and foot racing plus sack and wheelbarrow races. Prize monies were good, with first prizes ranging between ten shillings and £2, half to a full week's wages for a skilled craftsman at the time.

There was dancing in a marquee and at ten o'clock, the official Jubilee celebrations came to an end with a large bonfire on the top of Summerhouse Hill and from which it was reported over 60 celebration bonfires could be seen on surrounding hills.

The crowd at the opening of Sidney Gardens.

As darkness fell, Yeovil was illuminated by hundreds of candle fairy lights in coloured glass jars as well as oil and gas lamps. At the entrance to the Gas Works at the bottom of Middle Street there was a 'brilliantly illuminated arch surmounted by a Crown'.

Hundreds of townsfolk paraded the streets admiring the illuminations, the pubs had an hour's extension, and the *Western Gazette* wrote that 'It was gratifying to be able to report that everything went off pleasantly and that during the day no accident occurred and loyalty reigned supreme.'

28

BLUE ANCHOR HOLIDAY MEMORIES

T HE AUTHOR RECALLS the good times of his holidays at Blue Anchor in the 1940s.

Every year from 1942 to 1949, we went to Blue Anchor and spent the last week in July in one of the 'huts' which ran along the seaward side of the Taunton to Minehead railway line. The huts, which today would be called no doubt 'holiday chalets' or such like, had been placed on site between the two world wars and my father would rent one for a week. They followed a general layout, one big room, with double doors opening on to the beach, and a small kitchen; water was drawn from a stand-pipe, and for sanitation – a pail was used and emptied at the communal toilet at the entrance to the site! There were black huts, brown, green and white ones, ours was dark blue, but the one thing they had in common was that they were away from the cares of daily life and everyone was on holiday. Being so close to the railway line, in our case less than thirty feet, there was always the unforgettable smell of steam and the clanking of the wheels, as the train slowly passed to and from Minehead.

Until 1946, we used to travel to Blue Anchor by train and just before Watchet I would get my first glimpse of the sea and here the line passed the firing range where the Royal Air Force Regiment from Doniford camp trained its anti-aircraft gunners and for a boy, the first sight of the sea and the guns were equally thrilling. Little did I know that I would spend eight months of my RAF service at this light anti-aircraft gunnery school.

At the end of the war, limited supplies of petrol became increasingly available for private motoring, and the family Singer car, which had been put away for the duration of hostilities, was back on the road. In 1946 we drove to the hut but because petrol was still relatively scarce the car was

Blue Anchor Beach and Huts.

parked for the week in the Blue Anchor Garage, and all holiday journeys made by train or bus.

We used to get groceries from Greenslade's wooden shop near the railway station and collect our daily milk in a can from the dairy in the field next to the caravan park. At the end of the war, ice creams (Walls), usually in tubs or wafer blocks, could be bought from a wooden pavilion with a veranda, next to the communal lavatories – I can't recall any ill effects from the close proximity!

During the war years, the balloon barrage could be clearly seen flying over Barry on the other side of the Bristol Channel, and on some days the Bofors guns from the Doniford range would fill the sky with dirty grey puffs of bursting shells and the thud of explosions.

Along the coast, when invasion threatened in the early days of the war, hundreds of thick wooden poles were placed between the high and low water marks to discourage landing by glider-borne troops. At low tide many of the locals and holidaymakers would run fishing lines between the poles and tie on a dozen or so hooks which would be baited with lugworm and covered with mud or sand to protect the bait from hungry gulls. The lines would be covered by the tide and when it went out there was usually a catch of fish. We tried 'night lining', as it was called, but we were not very successful fishermen. We caught a few dogfish, but my mother refused to prepare them, as they resembled a small shark with skin like sandpaper, and had to be skinned before cooking.

When the tide disappeared into the distance there were some fine stretches of firm sand, ideal for the communal cricket matches of scores of fathers, boys and the occasional girl, for making sandcastles, building lakes and dams on the many rivulets, until swept clean again by the next tide. There was usually great fun when the tide came swirling in and slightly raised areas of sand would become islands on which we would allow our imaginations to run free until the islands began to disappear and we would run splashing back to dry land. The rock pools under the alabaster cliffs were a joy to explore, and we would collect limpets and winkles which my mother would boil for tea. I seem to recall that there was some sort of taste, but the texture seemed rather rubbery.

The fields on the other side of the railway line were good hunting grounds for my hobby of collecting butterflies. In the nineteen forties when butterflies and moths were so plentiful, many boys and girl collectors, caught and killed these beautiful creatures in a variety of ways (I used cotton wool sprinkled with ammonia placed in a sealed jam jar,) and then set them by spreading their wings on a block before displaying them. Armed with a jam jar, and my butterfly net made from old lace curtain material, a bamboo cane and a loop of chicken wire, I would set out into the fields to hunt Clouded Yellows, Painted Ladies, Gate Keepers, Red Admirals, Commas, Tortoise Shells and the occasional Marbled White, whilst in the coverts which extended towards Carhampton, Speckled Woods would dance in the shafts of sunlight.

We would walk across the 'butterfly' fields to Carhampton and I remember a thatched cottage on the Minehead road where we used to buy large golden plums. Sometimes we would go on the train to Minehead, and with it comes the memory of the occasional Knickerbocker Glory in an ice cream parlour on the front and the fascinating sounds from the amusement arcade in the main street by the cinema. How often are memories stirred by taste and sound, Dunster will always be associated with the taste of ginger beer drunk from a stone bottle and Blue Anchor with the gentle slap of small waves on the pebble beach in the early morning.

The huts have long gone but for me, the memory remains of many happy times spent at Blue Anchor a long time ago.

29

THE SATURDAY MORNING CINEMA CLUBS

ONE OF THE bright spots for many youngsters was the Saturday morning clubs at the Odeon and Gaumont cinemas.

On Saturday 5 June 1937, one month after the Yeovil Odeon was opened in Court Ash, the new Mickey Mouse Matinee Club opened with a feature film, news, a cartoon and episode one of the serial *The Phantom Rider* with Buck Rogers. The doors opened at 9.45 am, membership was free and club badges awarded after three weeks' attendance; admission three pence and sixpence for the balcony. Also, on Saturday morning 5 June 1937, the Gaumont British Kiddies' Club, of which the child star Shirley Temple was President, opened in the town's rival Gaumont cinema by the Triangle. Membership was free and cards to qualify could be obtained from the manager, at the pay box any weekday between 4.30 and 5.30 pm or at the children's matinee on Saturday mornings; admission sixpence.

Both clubs were enjoyed by hundreds of children until the dangerous days in the summer and autumn of 1940 when, with the threat of invasion from Nazi-occupied Europe and the bombing of our towns and cities, the Gaumont Kiddies' Club closed in July 1940 and in September, the Odeon Mickey Mouse Club closed until further notice.

On 10 April 1942, the Odeon's weekly advertisement of forthcoming films announced the re-opening of the Saturday morning Children's Club now renamed, the Odeon National Cinema Club for Boys and Girls.

However, the Gaumont's club remained closed until January 1945 when *Yeovil Review* reported:

'What should be of particular interest to boys and girls age 7 to 14 is the inauguration of the Gaumont Cinema Junior Club, which will open on

27 January. The idea is that the children shall meet socially every Saturday morning in a happy atmosphere, where educational and interesting films, "Secrets of Nature", Travel etc. will be introduced into Club programmes, after being carefully selected by a committee. In this respect, contact will be kept with the local education authorities. The children will be brought into contact with outstanding personalities from all walks of life – people who have distinguished themselves by their contribution to science, literature, art, by their service to their Country, or by their efforts for the benefit of mankind. In addition, there will be competitions which the club members will be encouraged to join, and every effort will be made to discover and develop individual talent in this direction. A scholarship scheme is under consideration. Outstanding feature is that the Club will be self-governing and self-disciplined, thus making members self-reliant by fostering a sense of responsibility and team spirit. Furthermore, the Club is non-profitmaking. All the receipts are used for the benefit of the Club

Young members of the Odeon Saturday Morning Cinema Club outside the cinema in 1947.

and its members. There is no membership fee, and the admission to Club meetings and film performances will be 6d. Every boy and girl joining will be issued with an official membership card. Last but not least, it is learned that a famous film star will visit the Gaumont Theatre, Yeovil, and officially open the Club on January 27th.'

The *Western Gazette* reported that the famous film star was – 'Jean Kent, the young Gaumont British star who has appeared in *"Fanny by Gaslight"* and *"Two Thousand Women"* and other films, and known to thousands of children as Auntie Jean, for she devotes her free Saturday mornings visiting Junior Clubs in various parts of the country.'

There were over 400 youngsters in the Gaumont on that Saturday morning 27 January 1945, when the Mayor Councillor W. S. Vosper, opened the inaugural meeting of the Club and told his young audience that in addition to the film shows, Mr Davey, the manager, was arranging for some very interesting people to come and talk to them. Mr Davey thanked the mayor, and read telegrams from Tommy Handley (of ITMA fame), Mr J. Arthur Rank, the club president, the Junior Clubs at Frome and Salisbury, and to applause, a telegram was read from their Majesties the King and Queen! Club Controller, Mr Victor Powel, addressed the young audience and after explaining the club's activities, he introduced the guest of honour, Jean Kent, alias Auntie Jean, who was presented with a bouquet by Margaret Etchells. Auntie Jean presented club badges to six members with birthdays on 27 January and then led the youngsters in community singing.

The author remembers spending many happy hours at the Saturday Morning Pictures, as they were called, and because members' birthdays were celebrated by free admission, many belonged to both the Odeon and Gaumont Clubs!

30

TAUNTON'S 'CORONATIA' FÊTE

August Bank Holiday Monday 7 August 1911, was the day chosen by the Taunton Carnival Committee for a 'Coronatia Fête' in Vivary Park. The Coronation of King George V had been held a few weeks previously on 22 June, and the Committee, reflecting the nationwide celebrations of the occasion decided that 'Coronatia' would be a very appropriate title for the Bank Holiday event.

The day dawned bright and breezy, just the weather for a successful fête. Besides the usual attractions of sideshows, stalls and refreshment tents, there was an 'aerial railway', a shooting gallery, an 'electricity stall', and a 'Hall of Laughter'. A 'trick cyclist' performed some amazing stunts, the May-pole dancing drew a large and appreciative crowd and four exhibitions of 'the entirely new game of basketball given by members of the Taunton Wesley Club was well-received by a mainly youthful audience.

However, the chief attraction was the advertised flights by Mr B. C. Hucks, in his monoplane. In 1911 aviation was in its early days and no doubt many of the people attending the fête had never seen any form of flying machine.

On Wednesday 9 August the *Taunton Courier* reporting the fête wrote that:

'The chief attraction was a monoplane flight by Mr B. C. Hucks, and this undoubtedly brought large crowds from the surrounding districts, for all the excursions running into the town were well patronised, whilst hundreds made the journey by road. Early in the day the Pilot gave two demonstrations to large crowds, and explained the various parts of his machine, which was the one he used in the recent *Daily Mail* race. He compared the monoplane to a biplane, and informed his audience that the latter machine was much safer for flights as it was fitted with two planes, one above the other, whilst the monoplane had only one. He also

Mr Bentfield Charles Hucks, the Aviator.

expressed the opinion that the ground was not suitable for flying, and unless he had a calm he could not make an ascent. Three flights were advertised, but only one took place. This, however, satisfied the people, for after seeing that flight they were quite content. Finding that he could not ascend in the Vivary lands, Mr Hucks had his machine run out out in Ash Meadows, where he was watched by a crowd of many thousand people. The machine was set in motion, and, after running along the ground for a short distance the monoplane rose gracefully into the air amidst loud applause. The flight however, was a short one, and the machine failing to rise to any great altitude came to ground in the second field. Mr Hucks had his machine taken back to the starting point and made a second attempt to fly. After a few minutes waiting the crowd saw the machine rise in the air, but once again it came to ground in the almost identical spot where it landed before. The descents on each occasion was very graceful, and the pilot brought his machine to a standstill with the greatest of ease. Finding it impossible to rise to a sufficient height from Ash Meadows Mr Hucks had his machine taken to a field a Cotlake Hill and from here got an ascent for what proved to be a splendid flight. Many people had not gone to the higher ground adjoining the Vivary Land, and the first intimation they received that a flight was taking place was the whirr of the engine, and within a few seconds they saw the machine glide gracefully over the trees. Mr Hucks encircled the grounds three or four times amidst tremendous applause, which he acknowledged whilst in the air. He descended with the greatest of ease at Ash Meadows, from which he was carried shoulder high surrounded by a jubilant throng, to the Vivary Lands. The crowd had witnessed a magnificent flight, and they were well pleased. The engine, which weighed on 150 lbs. consisted of seven cylinders, and was 50 h.p. The propeller makes one thousand revolutions per minute. After the flight the machine was brought back to the hangar and inspected by a large crowd.'

Mr Bentfield Charles Hucks was one of the nation's aviation pioneers and was the first Briton to perform a loop in an aircraft. When the First World War broke out in 1914 he joined the Royal Flying Corps but was sent home from the Western Front suffering from pleurisy and was subsequently invalided out. However, Bentfield Hucks' aviator's skills were not wasted and became a test pilot but sadly died aged 34 on 7 November 1918 just four days before the Armistice brought the war to an end on the eleventh, a victim of the Spanish Flu pandemic raging at the time.

31

THE BOROUGH CENTENARY

On Friday 9 July 1954, the *Western Gazette* reported that 'Yeovil has had a week of celebration which will be memorable in its modern history. They have been held in commemoration of the modern Corporation's centenary and have been enthusiastically supported by the people of the town and country. The proud record of the borough with its considerable progress and development in recent years was the subject of congratulation and comment by a number of the honoured guests who attended the opening ceremony on Saturday.'

The Centenary Celebrations of the establishment of the Yeovil Borough Council in 1854 began during the morning of Saturday 3 July with two parades to St John's church for the commemoration service. The Mayor's Civic procession, with the Yeovil Salvation Army Band at its head, left the Municipal Offices in King George Street

Mr D. G. Hiscott (left) and Mr E. R. Dunster of the Town Clerk's Department at the Yeovil Corporation's information desk at the Trades Fair.

and marched to the parish church by way of South Street, Hendford, Princes Street and Church Street. Meanwhile, the Services procession assembled in Newton Road and led by the Band of the Royal Marines Portsmouth, made its way through the streets and the crowds lining the route to St John's (one of the 500 who marched was the author as a member of the of Yeovil School's Army Cadet Corps).

At half-past two that afternoon, the Yeovil Trades Fair was opened in the grounds of Hendford Manor by Marshal of the Royal Air Force Sir John Slessor GCB DSO MC, who arrived in a Westland S-51 helicopter. All the principal manufacturers and businesses of the town were represented, with the emphasis on leather and glove making. During the afternoon, the Band of the Royal Marines played selections of popular music, and members of the Yeovil Business and Professional Women's Guild and ladies' section of Toc H dressed in period costumes of the 1850s sold programmes for the Old Yeovil Exhibition in Hendford Manor Hall.

The Southwestern section of the Veteran Car Club of Great Britain organised a rally of over 40 veteran cars in the Hendford Manor Paddock. Earlier in the afternoon the cars had left for Marston Magna to undertake driving tests, and returned to Yeovil via Rimpton, Adber and Mudford for the presentation of prizes.

Centenary Week continued with the Trades Fair opening daily from 11 a.m. to 8.30 p.m. with entertainment from the Yeovil Philharmonic Orchestra on Tuesday evening, The Rhine Staff Band of the Royal Tank Regiment on Thursday afternoon, and the Yeovil Corporation Silver Prize Band played on the closing Saturday evening.

The Westland Cine Society presented a film show and exhibition of cine equipment on Wednesday evening in a marquee at the Fair. Every seat was taken for the programme which included a cartoon, a film on helicopters, followed by a comedy.

By Wednesday afternoon, over 6800 people had visited the Fair.

Entertainment during the Week included a concert version of *Merrie England* performed by the Yeovil and District Amateur Operatic Society in the Princes Theatre on Sunday evening 4 July. Also in the Princes Theatre, Scott, Allan and Goodwin Productions presented *Dial M for Murder* nightly from 5 to 10 July. The famous Bertram Mill's Circus presented 'musical chimpanzees, world-renowned trapeze artists, a host of brilliant clowns and the amazing Borra, King of the Pick-Pockets', under the big-top in Barwick Park.

Following the re-organisation of the United Kingdom's local government structure on 1 April 1974 Yeovil Borough Council ceased to exist as an independent local authority after 120 years and was combined with seven neighbouring local authorities into the new Yeovil District Council, subsequently renamed South Somerset District Council. However, in 1982 the Yeovil Town Council was set up and administers a number of services in the town both in its own right and on behalf of the District Council.

32

TWO VICTORIAN WEDDING CELEBRATIONS

At Maperton

On Thursday 21 November 1867, the parish church of Maperton, near Wincanton, was the scene of the society wedding of Charlotte Elizabeth Harriet, the eldest daughter of Major H. T. G. Fitz-Gerald, of Maperton House, to Captain J. T. Coke. The *Western Gazette,* reporting on the occasion, wrote that:

'The bridal party proceeded from the residence of Major Fitz-Gerald to the church, which is close by, on foot, the pathway having been covered with cocoa-nut matting. The approaches to the church were lined with spectators, and the building itself was crowded by persons, principally young ladies, who were anxious to witness the ceremony. The church had been decorated with flowers and evergreens, and presented a very pretty appearance. The bride was led to the altar by her father, who also gave her away, and was accompanied by six bridesmaids, viz: – Miss Geraldine Fitz-Gerald, sister of the bride, Miss Munck, Miss Louisa Munck, Miss Fanny Munck, Miss Florence Wyndham, and Miss Clare Dickenson. Their dresses were of white grenadine, with scarlet violet trimmings, scarlet jackets with white goat's-hair fringe, and white bonnets with scarlet feathers. Each carried a splendid bouquet, composed of white and scarlet chrysanthemums bordered with scarlet, and frosted – margin maiden-hair fern. The bride wore a dress of white satin trimmed with swans down and d'Alencon lace, with pearl ornaments; lace veil, and wreath of orange blossoms, and carried a lovely bouquet, composed of white camellias and pink roses, bordered with frosted-margin maiden-hair fern. The whole of the bouquets were arranged by Mr Wallace, gardener to Major Fitz-Gerald. The bridegroom, Capt. J.T. Coke, was accompanied by Capt. Robertson of the 17th Lancers, who acted as "best man." He was attended by – Curtis-Hayward, Charles

Fitzgerald, Heathcote Wyndham, and Reginald Butterworth, who acted as groomsmen. Amongst those who were present at the breakfast were Colonel and Mrs Coke, Debdale Hall, Nottinghamshire; Mr and Mrs Fitzgerald, Lurlough Park; Colonel Mayo; Mr and Mrs Bligh; – Munck, Coley Park, Berks; Mrs. Wyndham, Yarlington House; Rev. and Mrs Moore, Hordley Rectory, Shropshire; Mr and Mrs Bowles; Miss Peal; Mrs Chatfield; Miss Drake; Miss Weatherton; Miss Kingswell; Capt. Robertson (17th Lancers); Capt. Curtis-Hayward (25th Regt.) Mr Newton-Dickinson (20th Regt.) Mr Reginald Butterworth, Mr Heathcote Wyndham, Mr Edward Wyndham, Rev. Calcraft Wylox, Rev. G. and Mrs Saunders, Mr Charles Fitz-Gerald, Mr Gerald Fitz-Gerald, &. The ceremony was performed by the Rev. G. Saunders, assisted by the Rev. S.W. Moore, uncle of the bride. The weather which has hitherto been so fine, proved unfavourable; but, although it was so gloomy, was not enough to damp the joy which was depicted on the countenance of the bridal party. As they issued from the church the bells burst forth a merry peal. The presents were very numerous, numbering over 120. The inhabitants of Maperton presented the bride with a very handsome silver cream-jug and sugar-basin, as a token of the respect which they entertain for her; and as she leaves them, she will be followed by many an earnest wish that the state of the weather may not be a criterion of what her future life will be; but that the sunshine of happiness may shine upon her throughout her married life, and that for once it may be said, "Happy indeed is the bride whom the sun did not shine upon."

At Bruton

The *Western Gazette* wrote that a stranger travelling through Bruton on a fine sunny morning in May 1870, would have wondered why the town was in festive mood. The shops were closed, arches of green foliage spanned the streets, flags hung from windows and banners were suspended over the entrance roads. Men and boys wearing rosettes of white ribbon and the womenfolk carrying bunches and garlands of flowers, thronged the town. The Union flag flew in the gentle breeze on the tower of St Mary's church and the bells rang out.

If the stranger had asked any of the rosette wearing Brutonians what was afoot, the reply would have been, 'Why, our respected land agent, Mr

Thomas Oatley Bennett's eldest son, Thomas, is getting married today to Miss Emma White of Coombe Hill House.' The stranger would also learn that Mr Bennett, junior, a land agent like his father, had gained the respect of all his neighbours by his general kindness, courteous behaviour and gentlemanly conduct. Also, he had exhibited kindness in doing all he could, to promote the interests and happiness of his neighbours, young and old, rich or poor. Likewise, Miss Emma, the eldest daughter of Bruton solicitor, Mt John R. White's four daughters, had won the esteem of her neighbours by her usefulness and unaffected kindness.

And so, the town of Bruton was preparing to give the popular couple a day to remember.

The weather was perfect, the sky was blue, the sun shone, and in the words of 'one enthusiastic dame', 'It sims as tho' th' day was send a'purpose.'

St Mary's church was packed with guests and spectators for a full hour before the ceremony, but at half-past eleven, the bridal party arrived in their carriages and the bride was led to the altar by her proud father accompanied by six bridesmaids.

Miss Emma wore a dress of white corded silk, trimmed with white satin, a veil of white lace with a band of orange blossom about her head and she carried a bouquet of white orange blossom. Her bridesmaids wore white grenadine dresses trimmed with white and green satin piping, bonnets of white tulle trimmed with fern and pink rosebuds, and white tulle veils.

At the conclusion of the ceremony, the happy couple walked from the church to their carriage along a path strewn with flowers by the children of the Church and National Schools.

The wedding breakfast was held at Coombe Hill House, and following a sumptuous meal and numerous speeches, the guests adjourned to the drawing room to view the many fine presents. One splendid silver centre piece consisted of two palm trees with slightly twisted trunks and bearing a glass dish. The palms stood on a massive base representing the earth, with various flowers, herbs etc, and on which also crouched two realistic model greyhounds. The base of the centre piece bore the following inscription – *Presented to T.O. Bennett, junr., by the members of the Hadspen and Shepton Montague Coursing Club, as a token of their esteem and friendship, on the occasion of his marriage – 18th May 1870.*

There was also a fine silver salver given by the tradesmen of Bruton.

The children of the Church, Independent, and Wesleyan Sunday Schools, formed up near St Mary's, and with a brass band in the lead, possessed to Coombe Hill House where they marched around the lawn cheering and waving flags.

Tea was laid out for the children and their parents in a marquee in a nearby field where swings and various amusements were provided for the youngsters. A brass band, directed by Mr Rumsey of Shepton Mallet, played a selection of tunes throughout the afternoon.

Bruton was in festive mood for the wedding in May 1870.

Meanwhile, Mr Bennett, senior, treated the church choir and a number of townspeople to a fine luncheon in the church schoolroom.

Following the wedding breakfast, the guests inspected the wedding presents, and as the bride and groom left to honeymoon in the Lake District, their carriage was showered with slippers as it was driven down the drive.

The festivities at Coombe Hill House continued into the early hours of the following morning accompanied by the music of Mr Rumsey's quadrille brass band.

Bruton had thoroughly enjoyed itself, and the wedding of Mr Thomas Bennett, junior, and Miss Emma White, would almost certainly be remembered for many years to come!

33

SIX DAYS OF FUN

'Six Days of Fun' was how the *Western Gazette* described Yeovil Carnival Week when it opened on Monday 14 November 1949.

Nineteen-years-old Jane Harris, from Aberdeen, a WREN serving at the Royal Naval Air Station Yeovilton, was chosen Carnival Queen by film star Hy Hazel, at a ball in the Liberal Club, with Jean Hockey (Miss West Coker) and Brenda Pearce (Miss Yeovil) selected as the Queen' two Princesses. Following the ceremony, bouquets were presented to Hy Hazel and the Mayor and Mayoress (Alderman and Mrs Ben Dening) by Phyllis Consitt, daughter of the Carnival Secretary, and over 700 danced to the music of the Commodore Ballroom Orchestra.

Carnival Week began with a Monday evening Variety Concert in the Princes Ballroom at the Princes Street Assembly Rooms followed on Tuesday by an 'Olde Tyme Carnival Dance' organised by the Yeovil Gay Nineties Club. The Commodore Olde Tyme Orchestra provided the music and the 200 or so dancers were occasionally showered with balloons and fancy hats.

The Yeovil Literary and Dramatic Society presented two one-act plays *Hullabaloo* and *Two Gentlemen of Soho* in the Princes Ballroom. Between performances, there were dancing displays by the Yeovil Central School of Dancing and the evening's entertainment attracted an audience of nearly 400 patrons.

On Thursday evening the Mayor's Carnival Ball was held in the Liberal Club on Middle Street (tickets at 15 shillings double and 10 shillings single) and Noel Gulliver compered 'Opportunity Knocks' in the Princes Ballroom. There were over 20 contestants ranging from one-string fiddlers to paper tearers, from eccentric comedians to impressionists. Two accordionists from Houndstone Army camp, John Priddey and Trevor Lee, won first prize and a special award went to Petty Officer Norman Davidson described as an eccentric comedian.

'Youth Takes a Bow' was held in the Princes Ballroom on Friday evening and was billed as 'A variety entertainment organised by Youth Organisations of Yeovil and District featuring St Johns's Gym and the Milborne Port Girls' Choir.' There was an under 18's 'Opportunity Knocks' won by 14-years-old George King of Milborne Port after a 'sing-off' with Yeovil's Christine Tavener. The *Western Gazette* reported that 'Two young accordionists Alistair Rollo of Fielding Road and Gerald Purchase, Rosebery Avenue, came third, and a 17-years-old pianist Don Rogers, Cromwell Road, received a special award.' George Patterson, Yeovil Town Football Club's Player Manager, went on stage and congratulated the contestants on their high standard.

Friday evening also saw a Whist Drive, sponsored by the Ladies Whist League, at the Labour Club on Vicarage Street.

However, Saturday was the big day, and in the early evening, the mayor crowned Jane Harris, Carnival Queen, in the Borough and, accompanied by her two Princesses and 12 attendants, she was driven in style on the back of a 'charmingly decorated lorry' to Rosebery Avenue, where the 92 carnival entries had assembled. At 6.30 sharp, with the familiar figure of Mr Edwin (Tinker) Robbins mounted on his trusty steed at its head, the procession moved off to wend its way through St Michael's Avenue, Matthews Road, Eastville, Southville, up Reckleford to Higher Kingston, Preston Road, St Andrew's Road, Preston Grove, Huish, Westminster Street, High Street, down Middle Street to disperse in Wyndham Street. The *Western Gazette* reported that:

'Thousands of cheering spectators lined the two-mile long route which was blanketed in fog, but the glare from the torches and the countless coloured fairy lights of the tableaux helped dispel the gloom. Lighting was an outstanding feature of the procession and many of the tableaux were equipped with their own generating plant either concealed or trailer drawn. The fact that this year there were 92 entries, almost double last year's number, illustrated the popularity of, and support generally given to the carnival. All the necessary ingredients of a successful carnival – music, mirth, colour, majesty, and even drama – were displayed.

A Patriotic Carnival Float.

'It was a great occasion too, for the newly formed Yeovil Town band, who got off to a most auspicious start. There was no lack of music, for bands from Shaftesbury, Kingsbury, the R.N. Air Station, Yeovilton, as well as the Boys' Brigade, A.T.C. and A.C.F., Yeovil, were also "on parade".

'There were plenty of good humoured but embarrassing situations before the "Mystery Man" was correctly challenged by Miss Ann Collins, of the N.A.A.F.I., Yeovilton.

'Most popular class in the carnival was that for juvenile pedestrians, but entries were also numerous in the motor tableaux and trade groups. The intricate marshalling and moving off of the precision proved a triumph of organisation. The ready assistance and co-operation of the Services at Houndstone and Yeovilton was evident, and all along the route collectors kept spectators light in spirit and endeavoured to make them light of pocket.'

With 92 entries it would take up too much space to record them all, but here are a few to give a taste of the show: Relief of the Lighthouse, Bisto Kids,

Dodum Cow, Pied Piper of Chard, Comic Motor Car Group by the newly formed Yeovil Car Club, The Courshay Kids Juvenile Circus featuring the Hawkchurch Young Liberals, Fresh v Dried Milk by Yeovil Young Farmers Club, The Modern Army, Trent Comic Fire Brigade, Rickshaw Boys, RNAS Yeovilton Fire Fighting Mess, RNAS Yeovilton's model of the new aircraft carrier HMS *Triumph* on a 60-foot trailer dressed overall in fairy lights, Housewives on Strike, and Crackers.

The Carnival Cup, the premier trade award was won by Yeovil Co-operative Society's 'Christmas Fare' displaying Co-operative goods, with a life-like Father Christmas and his reindeer on the roof. Yeovil Sports Club's 'Indian Pageantry' won first prize in the senior tableaux class and 'Snow White and the Seven Dwarfs' won the juniors'.

After the procession, a fireworks display was held on the Yeovil School playing field in Mudford Road, at which the combined bands of the Air Training Corps and the Army Cadet Corps provided the musical entertainment. Admission was one shilling adult, children under 15, six pence, and free entry to badge-wearing members of the *Bristol Evening Post's* Pillar Box Club.

The Grand Carnival Dance in the Princes Ballroom brought the 'Six Days of Fun' to an end and at midnight on 19 November 1949, like Cinderella at the close of the ball, Yeovil returned to normal.

34

SONG AND DANCE IN DECEMBER 1972

Looking back to December 1972 and at some of the local entertainments advertised in Somerset newspapers.

Western Gazette

On Friday 8 December, BRIAN DAY appeared at Maggie's Club in Yeovil's Court Ash, followed the next evening by SHAFT. GREEN STEAM performed on the following Friday, Saturday was CRYSTAL's turn and on Sunday STUART HUGHES presented his DISCO (with fantastic light show). Friday 22 December saw CORE providing the entertainment; the Christmas Special on the 23rd presented FOXY. The ELECTRIC BATH saw Maggie's into Christmas Day.

Another of Yeovil's popular night clubs, Carnaby's in Tabernacle Lane, presented HONEY SUCKLE and Resident DJ on Saturday and Sunday 9 and 10 December, on Tuesday, the 12th, there was DISCO SCENE '72 followed on Thursday by OVER 21'S PARTY NIGHT with the CONCORDS. The HOLLY BALL on 20 December, featuring the RAY COX ORCHESTRA plus BERNARD PLANT (Mr Melody & Mirth), completed the Christmas entertainment.

In Yeovil's hotels, there was Saturday evening dine and dance in the Three Choughs on Hendford from 8 until midnight, appearing at the Westfield Hotel on 23 December were The Fabulous HARLEQUIN ACES, and the 'Ever Popular HARMONY & SLIDE' on Boxing Night. It was Steak and Skittle Nights every Friday and Saturday at the Greyhound Hotel on South Street. Yeovil Sports Club advertised a Grand New Year's Eve Dance at Johnson Park with the DANCE SCENE and the STUART HUGHES DISCO.

Another popular venue was the Rum Hole at the Coker Motel, West Coker, where you could dine and dance by candlelight to the MARK WARD TRIO on 10 December.

Central Somerset Gazette

Every Saturday evening at the Star Hotel, Wells, in addition to the Traditional Christmas Fare, there would be 'live music' with the 'Resident Hostess Pat Rycroft' looking after patrons during the festive season.

Meanwhile, Street's Unity Club's Christmas attractions included THE AVALON BAND and THE TWO J's, GIRL TALK DUO and JACK SYMES. The CONCORDS featured on Christmas Eve followed by the BEE TONES at the Windmill Club on Boxing Day evening.

Somerset Standard

At the Lamb Inn, Clandown, prospective patrons were invited to come and enjoy 'your Boxing Night and New Year's Eve' with STRINGS ATTACHED and on Christmas Eve ROY was at the piano. If you were living in the Frome area, DEREK JAMES invited you through the advertising feature in the *Somerset Standard* to join him at an evening DISCO-DINE, every Friday at the Mendip Hotel and at his OLD-YEAR DISCO DANCE on the 28 December. Frome Rugby Club's Boxing night dance featured EMPIRE plus DJ. Frome Youth Centre-Pre School Playgroup's supper dance (adults only) in the Youth Centre on Vallis Road featured 'Dancing to THE BENNY PASSMORE SOUNDS'.

In the Farrington Gurney Memorial Hall, the Welton Rovers Social Club held their Christmas Dance on 16 December to the music of THE ATLANTIC DANCE BAND.

Cheddar Valley Gazette

BERNIE DOOLAN SOUNDS FOR ALL OCCASIONS presented his Disco in Glastonbury Town Hall on 2 December and every Wednesday His Sounds for all Occasions featured at The Pilgrims Rest, Lovington.

On the municipal scene, the RAYMOND KAYE DIPLOMATES played for the Glastonbury Borough Council's End of Year Ball at the Town Hall on Friday 29 December.

Wells Journal

Every Saturday evening from 8 pm to midnight there was DUNGEON DISCO at Mr Chef, Cannards Grave, admission 30p, minimum age 18 years and 'Sorry no Leather Jackets'.

The Rum Hole, West Coker.

Now under the title D.J. BERNIE DOOLAN, he was back at Glastonbury for one night only on Saturday 23 December in the St Louis Convent school on Magdalene Street (the school closed after nearly 60 years in 1984).

At the Weston-super-Mare Pavilion, THE STRAWBS were in concert on 23 December, and on Boxing Day couples took to the floor 'Christmas Dancing – Ballroom Style' to the SQUADS SHOWBAND.

Street's Royal British Legion Club's Christmas entertainment included Boxing Day dancing to THE LEGIONNAIRES from 9 pm to 1.30 am and on Saturday 30 December, COLIN DAY AND HIS MUSIC played from 8.30 to 11.45 pm.

FELICITY HAZE Guitar and Vocalist, entertained at the Strode Arms, Cranmore, from 8 to 11 pm on Saturday evening 9 December.

And finally, here are some of the other DJs, groups and bands entertaining the Somerset festive crowds in December 1972 – DANCE SOUND INCORPORATED, DEREK JAMES and TUESDAY, THE SKYLINERS, GEORDIE AND DEREK JAMES, BLACKFOOT SUE and the DAVE SCOTT DISCO, SOUNDS OF FIVE, and FLESH!

35

MISTLETOE, PRIZES AND A SUMPTUOUS SPREAD

For the people of Martock during the middle years of the 19th century, the appearance of horse and carts drawing up outside the railway station and off-loading their loads of mistletoe was confirmation that the Christmas season had well and truly begun. The *Western Flying Post* in its edition of 25 January 1859 explains where the mistletoe was going.

'Immediately before Christmas no less than twenty tons of mistletoe were conveyed on the Bristol and Exeter lines on its way to the London market. This interesting commodity was chiefly procured in the neighbourhood of Martock, Langport, &c. It was conveyed in eight trucks, each truck containing two-and-a-half-tons. We used to be amazed at the statistical fact

The Three Choughs Hotel (on the right of the image) circa 1899.

that the Cockneys spent £10,000 a-year on water-cresses, but what must be that wonderful capital which has twenty tons of kissing-bushes to order from one locality alone, for we presume there is hardly a railway which runs to the Metropolis that did not bear a stock of this article to London for the festive season. It would be a nice arithmetical question, which it makes one's lips water to work out, to calculate the amount of kissing that must have taken place under the supply sent from the West of England alone.'

Continuing with the agricultural theme, just before Christmas 1858, the Yeovil Agricultural Society held its annual dinner in the Three Choughs Hotel, and the occasion was accompanied by speeches, toasts and the distribution of prizes for the best cattle, sheep, pigs and breeding stock; prizes were also awarded for human activity as recorded by the *Western Flying Post*, and which included:

'PRIZES TO THE LABOURERS

'To the Labourer in Husbandry, with a good character, in the employ of a Member of the Society by whom the greatest number of legitimate children, (not less than five) shall have been brought up to at least seven years of age, in habits of honest industry, and who shall at no time have received parochial relief, except in sickness, a Society's Coat and Buttons, and £2 – To Thomas Prince, servant to Mr George Salter, Coombe Farm, for having brought up 11 children, and having been employed by his present master and predecessor for 31 years.

'To the Labourer in Husbandry, who shall have lived in the Family, or continued in the service or employ of a Member of the Society, or his or her predecessors, in the same Farm, with a good character, the greatest number of successive years (but not less than ten), and who shall not at any time have received parochial relief, except in sickness, a Society's Coat and Buttons, and £1 – To William Lane, servant to Mr Robert Templeman, Perrott, for 35 years.'

There were other rewards granted for long service to menservants and farm boys, carters, shepherds and two women servants, Ellen Lane and Martha James.

The *Flying Post* recorded that after the prizes had been dispensed – 'The Chairman having addressed the labourers in a brief but appropriate manner, Mr Udall proposed "three cheers for the honest and industrious Labourers," which were given with right good will.'

Forty-four years later in December 1899 and still continuing with the agricultural theme, dealers in the Yeovil cattle market held their Christmas Dinner in the Three Choughs Hotel and over 80 sat down to 'a most sumptuous spread of the best Christmas fare'. Toasts were drunk and speeches made. Mr John Sawtell on behalf of the dealers thought that 'the year was ending much better than it began and taking the good with the bad, there was not much to grumble about.' Another guest, Mr Samuel Harding believed the Christmas trade had been good and would wind up all right. However, a grazier, Mr Fred Miles was not so sure and said that 'the year had been the worst he ever knew, for during the summer the fields were almost bare of grass as the room in which they were seated, and the stock had to be fed with artificial food, which of course meant a great loss. The good prices realised lately, however, had mended a little of the damage,' he concluded.

And still in Yeovil in 1899 but this time with the meat trade in focus, on 22 December the front page of the *Western Gazette* carried an advertisement placed by Mr J.J. Brook of 6 Middle Street, describing himself as 'The Oldest Established Butchering Business in the Town' and advertising his 'Prime Prize Christmas Meat – Primest Devon Ox Beef, Exmoor and Down Wether Mutton and a Splendid Lot of Geese, Turkeys and Game at Prices Defying Competition' and declaring that 'The Best is Cheapest.'

However, if you were feeling the effects of sampling too much of Butcher Brook's seasonal fare you could rush off to your local chemist and purchase some of Short's Pleasant Pills 'most agreeable to take and a most effectual remedy for biliousness, sickness, constipation and liver complaints' in response to the advertisement on the same page of the *Western Gazette*.

36

OLD CHRISTMAS TIME

Christmas Day at the Chard Workhouse in 1887 was probably better than in many poor homes in the town. The *Western Gazette* wrote that 'Thanks to the liberality of the Guardians and the kindness of Mr and Mrs Pallin [the Master and Matron], the inmates spent a very enjoyable time on Christmas Day and Boxing Day.' The chapel was decorated with holly and ivy, a decorated Cross of Christmas Berries was hung over the Communion table, and on the walls were displayed the words 'Emmanuel, God with us'. After the service on Christmas Day, the 'inmates' enjoyed tea and cake, but the real festivities were held on Boxing Day. The Boxing Day dinner was served at 2 p.m. and consisted of prime roast beef, baked and boiled potatoes, together with a pint of beer for each adult inmate. An ounce of tobacco was given to each man, snuff to the old ladies, and oranges and sweets to the children. Cake, with bread and butter, was served for tea which was followed by a 'capital magic lantern display given by Mr Lucas and which was thoroughly enjoyed by young and old'. After the show, some ancient ditties were sung by the old people, who also got up and danced, and the *Gazette* reported that 'one old lady in particular (70 years of age) was very active and evidently had her young days over again'.

Just after Christmas in 1887, the Wincanton Cricket Club presented their annual concert in the Town Hall before the 'usual large and fashionable audience'. The wall behind the platform was covered with the Cricket Club's flag placed in the centre of two Union Jacks and the orchestra, conducted by Mr F. Wentworth-Bennett, were dressed in the red and white striped costumes of the Club and 'presented quite a gay appearance'. There was a full programme of orchestral and vocal numbers, and Mr W. Hardwick gained the first encore of the evening for his song *They all love Jack* and to which he responded by singing *True till Death.* Mr R. Hutchings appeared dressed in the uniform of the Wincanton Fire Brigade and sang a humorous song *The Fireman* which was loudly applauded. The evening was judged to have been a complete success and lived up to its reputation as one of the events of the season.

Five years later the Wincanton Church of England Temperance Society, held its Christmas Party in 1892 in the Parish Room where some forty members enjoyed a 'Very jolly evening playing chess, dominoes, draughts, Tiddle de Wink, Bogieman and various card games. Great hilarity was displayed over the scientific game of Tip the Button.' The evening was such a success, that everyone hoped it would be repeated before long.

At Crewkerne Christmas 1890 was described as being in keeping with the 'Good Old Days' and was very cold with snow lying inches deep on the town, the blanket of white reflecting the lights from the 'unusually attractive shop windows which added to the spirit of the Festive Season'. On Christmas Eve, the Town Band played through the snow-covered streets and Christmas Day was ushered in by parties of carol singers touring the town. Christmas Day services were held in the parish church, which was decorated throughout with holly and ivy, and during the afternoon the choir gave a recital of carols.

In Bruton the Old Bull Club held its annual dinner on 23 December 1890 in the Club Room of the Old Bull. A large gathering of members sat down to a 'capital dinner put on the table by Host Steeds'. Following numerous toasts, there were songs and recitations and a very enjoyable evening was had by all.

Over at North Brewham, Mr Duck's Dancing Class held a 'Long Night' in the village Assembly Room on Boxing Night of 1891. Dancing commenced at eight o'clock in the evening, and 'was kept up with spirit until four o'clock in the morning'. The Brewham Festive Season of 1892 included an evening's entertainment in the National Schoolroom given by the Bruton Blackbirds in aid of the church organ fund; Mr Haytor acted as conductor and Mrs Haytor provided the piano accompaniment. The farce *Starvation* was also performed to the full house.

In 1893 Somerton's Amateur Minstrels presented their popular Christmas show in the Town Hall, and the *Western Gazette's* correspondent wrote that 'The talent of this popular troupe and the classes of performance they give drew together a "good house" and the band was in excellent form.' The pieces performed included – *Hobbity Bobbity* – *Barney take me Home* – *Pollie Pie Crust* – *We're all Humbugs* – *I can tell it by your bumps* and concluded with the nostalgic song *I'll take you home again Kathleen*, which over a half a century later was sung by the Sons of the Pioneers in the 1950 film *Rio Grande* starring John Wayne and Maureen O'Hara.

The following article was published in *Pulman's Weekly News* on Tuesday 1 January 1895 and opens a glimpse to the seemingly gentler time of Christmas 1894 in the village of Trent near Sherborne. Although Trent is now in Dorset, the village was in Somerset at Christmas 1894 just before it was transferred over the border by a boundary change.

Trent Village School.

'Christmas-eve promises to be well-remembered by the school children of the parish [Trent], a fine Christmas-tree having been prepared for them by the kindness of the present temporary occupants of the Rectory, assisted by members of the congregation. The preparations commenced some three weeks before Christmas when a working party was held at the Rectory to furnish garments for a number of unusually pretty-faced dolls, and the young people who worked appeared to enter heartily into the undertaking knowing what pleasure they were preparing for the intended recipients. Other gifts were contributed in the shape of work-bags, cuffs, comforters, handkerchiefs, toys and sweetmeats, many of the parishioners having at their own accord sent contributions for the tree. The bulk of the articles, however, including work-boxes and scissors for the older girls, knives and books for the bigger boys, came from outside Trent. At six-o'clock on Christmas-eve the school was quite filled with all the day and Sunday scholars, besides many of their parents and friends. The exhibition commenced with Christmas hymns, and recitations of the story of the birth of Jesus Christ from the Gospel of St Luke by a child about eight years old, who repeated it clearly without missing a word. The Rev. H. Stern then addressed the children, pointing out in a few words the typical meaning of the tree and how it was the emblem of the Gospel with its many fruits of blessing. The tree was meanwhile lighted up, and presented a very bright appearance, covered with many pretty ornaments, some of the gaily-dressed dolls, and other gifts, the remainder being placed on a table below. Each child received a small gift, together with an orange, and a bag of sweets, and many young hearts were made glad.'

37

GOING A-WASSAILING

A CONTRIBUTION FROM *The Somerset Year Book 1939* published by The Society of Somerset Folk: 'Let's go a Wassailing! It's an old-time cider custom in Somerset "where the cider apples grow." We like our "drap o' zider," so to make sure of a good crop of apples we forgather every year on Old Twelfth Night (January 17th) at the village inn, the landlord of which has his own orchard and firmly believes in carrying out the customs of his forefathers. Sounds of merriment proceeding from the bar-room as we approach tell us that things are beginning to warm up, and as we enter we are greeted with choruses of those undying songs which are so dear to the heart of country folk. In spite of some of the younger element, who try to introduce "The Lambeth Walk" or some of the latest dance-hall ditties, the old-timers have their way, and "Little Brown Jug" is their favourite, while one about a contented farmer, with a chorus that runs;

> "While I've brown bread, home-brewed,
> And my cottage well thatched with straw,"

… is certainly the next in popularity.

'Farmer folk, each with his shot-gun and a pocket full of cartridges drift in, and have one "for luck" whilst waiting for the real business of the evening. Preparations are being made, jars are being filled with cider, and a brimming wooden pail of the same beverage appears. An old huntsman in his time, the landlord appears with the hunting horn, and a rousing blast calls the revellers to attention. He precedes the procession to the orchard, carrying the pail in one hand and a piece of toasted bread in the other.

'Here we gather round the oldest tree, up which with all solemnity, the youngest boy present climbs or is hoisted; a bowl of cider is dipped from the pail, the toast is dipped into it, and the lad places it into the fork of the tree, while the liquor is poured over the roots. A relic of ancient tree-worship this, the food and the libation being a propitiary offering to the gods.

'Now comes the "Wassail Song." There are many versions of this, but in our part of the country the following is still sung, as our forefathers sang it;

> "Old Apple Tree, Old Apple Tree,
> We be come to Wassail Thee,
> To bear and to bow apples enow;
> Hats full! Caps full! Three bushel bags full!
> Barns full! And a little heap under the stairs!
> Hip Hip Hurrah!"

'The Wassail song finished, the guns are raised and volleys fired into the branches, this having the effect of scaring away all the imps of evil which infest the tree; the pail of cider is then passed round, cups dipped into it, and everyone drinks to the future crop.

Wassailing the apple trees at Carhampton in the early 1930s.

'The young folk of the village, while not allowed in the bar-room of course, look forward eagerly to the orchard festivities and they must also have their sip of the Wassail-cup. A story is told of one village where Wassailing was a great yearly event. A few nights before the 17th a Band of Hope meeting was held for the children, who were then and there urged to sign the pledge to abstain from drinking alcohol]. They one and all refuse point-blank, with this proviso; "Not till after Wassailing!"

'In another village a startling climax occurred. When several Wassailers raised their guns, pointed them skyward through the branches of the apple-tree and fired a volley, there was a loud squawking and several fowls which had been roosting there were brought to the ground. The tale is still told also of a party of revellers who had visited a number of orchards and imbibed so freely of the liquor that they could not tell "t'other from which," and ended up by solemnly wassailing a lilac bush!'

The anonymous village with the landlord's orchard and the enjoyable Wassail was Carhampton near Minehead.

38

A WEEK OF PANTOMIMES 1951 AND 'MOTHER GOOSE' 1953

On 26 January 1951 the *Western Gazette* wrote that:

'For more than a week Yeovil audiences have been enjoying a pantomime produced by local organisations. A three-day run of "Cinderella" by St Andrew's Scouts and Guides, in St John's Schoolroom, at the end of last week was followed on Monday, with presentations all this week of "Robin Hood and the Babes in the Wood," by the Wessex Social and Sports Club, in the Assembly Rooms.

'That these local organisations were filling a need in the town was evidenced by the large audiences which they attracted, the Wessex Club, for instance, having had over 2000 advance bookings when they opened on Monday.

'More ambitious in its scope and lavishness than any of their previous pantomimes, "Robin Hood and the Babes in the Wood," reflects the greatest credit on an enterprising amateur company.

'The quality of the club's three earlier productions has assured Yeovil's own pantomime week of a place in local theatrical circles and a following as large and enthusiastic as that for ventures of the longer established operatic society.

'Before the doors of the Assembly Rooms opened for the first night on Monday, more than 2000 people had booked in advance the full floor seating capacity for the seven performances this week. A limited number of tickets for accommodation on the secondary stage, on sale at the door have been eagerly claimed each evening.

'A cast of nearly 50, almost all of them employees of the Southern Electricity Board's offices and workshops at Yeovil, professionally made costumes and scenery, lively dialogue studded with references to

Ninesprings and well-known Yeovil personalities, and excellent music treatment by an augmented orchestra directed by Harry Lawson, combine to make a memorable show. Not to be outdone in spectacle by their professional contemporaries of the cities and seaside resorts, an aerial ballet of male "fairies" has been introduced, and even a motor-car makes a appearance on the stage!

'The venture is a personal triumph for Mr W.B. Consitt, the producer and director, who was also responsible for the troupe's "Aladdin" last year. Free of the confines of St Joseph's Hall – venue of all their previous pantomimes – which imposed a severe handicap on presentation as well as accommodation, he has made full use of the improved staging facilities available.

'While conditions are not ideal for such a production, particularly behind the scenes, we have laboured for many weeks to make this hall as pleasant and comfortable as possible for audience and cast alike." Mr Consitt told a representative of the paper. Due to heavy production costs, Mr Consitt said it would not be possible, this year, to devote the proceeds of one performance to charity. "We had to play to full houses in order to clear ourselves," he explained.

'Following her success as Aladdin last year, principal boy Delores Carter well merits the confidence shown in her and makes an admirable Robin Hood. Eileen Matthews, playing her third successive leading role, is also charming as Maid Marion. Their voices are heard to good effect, particularly in the duet "I only have eyes for you." Mary Friend and Maureen Giles do well as the babes; while the effervescent stage personality of their nurse, Don Spinner, accounts for much of the show's mirth. Michael Budden (Coppernob), and Doug Smith (Gingernut), display their fine sense of villainous fun, their farcical antics with pantomime cow (Dave Ledger and Pete Burton) being a delight to children of all ages.

'Ron Pilkington, as the scheming baron works hard for the children's hisses – and gets them. Cyril Auton makes a convincing crusader knight, and Ken Dover an adequate landlord. Ken Hallett (Little John), Graham Score (Allan-a-dale), and Bert Hill (Friar Tuck), ably lead the "Merry Men of Sherwood Forest." Gladys Miller as the musical fairy, also does well. Others taking part are Wilf Fishburn (Sheriff), and his attendant Val Johns, Bert Jennings (The King) and Mick Stanley (Court Jester).

'Contributions by 13-year-old boy soloist Edward Priddle were a pleasant surprise. Good chorus work is provided by Doreen Ash, Joan Edgerley, Val Johns, Michael McDonald, Joan Shackell, Pete Burton, Frances Hodges, June Knight, Frank Parsons, Mary Watkins, Dennis Dover, Pat Johns, Maureen Mullaney, Ivy Pilkington, Phyllis Wilmot.

'Eleven little elves who charm with their singing and dancing are; Madeline Chubb, Pauline Gay, Christine Ishmael, Pauline Chubb, Joan Hayter, Christine Tetlow, June Courts, Carol Ishmael, Margaret Wilmot and dancers Heather Collins and Heather Lucas.

'A comical aerial ballet complete with "flying saucer" and an oscillating aeroplane, is one of the highlights. Taking part in this speciality act are Fed Hallett (Fairy Queen) D. and K. Dover, M. Ledger, G. Score and M. Stanley.

'Stage Manager is Len Miller, and others assisting behind the scenes are Ted Bond and Ken Parsons (stage electricians), Tom Samways (business manager) and Miss M. Young and F. J. Riches (make-up) Tubular scaffolding was specially erected for the aerial ballet by Mr Eric Botham, son of Mr V. C. Botham (the Southern Electricity Board's district engineer) and Mr J. B. Hodges was responsible for sound amplification. Dresses for the male fairies were made by Mrs B. Jennings and those for the two little ballet dancers by Mrs Q. Gay.'

The *Western Gazette* then went on to describe the St Andrew's Scouts and Guides' pantomime 'Cinderella':

'For the third year running the St Andrew's Scouts and Guides have given an unpretentious but thoroughly enjoyable pantomime. Following "Aladdin" and "Snow White" they, this year, turned to what is one of the best loved of all fairy tales – "Cinderella" – and on Thursday, Friday and Saturday, at St John's Schoolrooms, large audiences watched the ultimate triumph of modest Cinders over her noisy and over confident stepsisters.

'While the presentation never wandered too far from the original story, there were a number of novel touches and there was an air of freshness about the old plot. The young cast showed a commendable knowledge of the words and what was a slight lack of verve among one or two was readily disregarded because of the pace and assurance of the production as a whole.

'There was a generous measure of comedy – and if anything some of the slapstick was carried out a little too realistically! Audrey Lang had the title role and the Ugly Sisters were played with great gusto by Janie Finch and Richard Little. Frank Jenkin made a delightful Baron Slightly, while Tom Loudwill effectively made the most of his part of Choddles.

'As the principal boy, Kathleen Goodland was a neat, trim figure and put over her lines and songs in a pleasant manner. A good portrayal of Dandini, the Court dandy was given by Josie Tucker.

'Particularly enjoyed was the hilarious scene in the sisters' dressing room as they laboriously prepared for the Royal Ball. The musical accompanist was Ken Rawlings who had assisted with the musical side of the production.

'Other players were: – Brian Hunt, Jean Belcher, Wendy Blackburn, Patricia Roadhouse, Eileen Carradine and Peter Cutler. Fairies were: – Mary Sercombe, Astrid Major, Joyce Cregan and Ruth Belcher, and Freda Goodland was the coach driver. Between the scenes 10-year-old Roy Wheadon gave piano accordion solos.'

Two years later on 16 January 1953, the *Western Gazette* reviewed the Wessex (Yeovil) Social and Sports Club's sixth annual pantomime 'Mother Goose' presented at the Assembly Rooms now known as the Princes Theatre:

'Weeks of feverish preparation, the fear, doubts and mishaps of rehearsal, the last-minute cuts and alterations, ended last (Thursday) night for the cast of the Wessex (Yeovil) Social and Sport's Club's sixth annual pantomime, "Mother Goose," when their nine days run at the Princes Theatre, Yeovil, opened.

'As with most productions "everything seemed to come right in the end" and the result was an evening of vivacious and enthusiastic entertainment, encompassing all the traditional frolics of pantomime from the Dame to the Demon King.

'The cast managed to extract laughs in all the right places and Trudy West's script, with additional comedy and lyrics by Douglas Smith, who also took the part of the Demon King, was funny without the help of "blue" jokes or doubtful situations. Producer W.R. Consitt can be proud of his achievement in polishing a crowd of once-a-year actors and actresses into a smooth-running team, and the easy flow of dialogue and song was a credit.

The cast of Mother Goose.

'Perhaps the most successful aspect of the show, however, was the musical side, and Valerie Stead, who also danced, can take a bow for her choreography. The chorus, mainly composed of youngsters, had a fine sense of rhythm and were in good voice. Especially effective was the dance of the demons, which was extremely well done, with the expert aid of Bert Kerley's lighting and the music of the augmented orchestra directed by Harry Lawson.

'Comedy was also well catered for, Fred Laws, as Mother Goose, was broadly funny and was assisted with much gnashing of teeth and cracking of whip by Cyril Auton, as the wicked squire. The knock-about element was provided by Michael Budden with a new and highly amusing partner, Sydney Amatt. They were, of course, the bailiffs.

'But perhaps the funniest of all was the scene in which a group of rather awkward and bony-legged aspiring ballerinas, suitably garbed, burlesqued a ballet lesson during which they nearly drive their teacher (Valerie Stead) to distraction.

'One must not forget the love interest, attractively served up by Jean Dover (Sam), Pauline Ratcliffe (Susie), Eileen Matthews (Jill), Delores

Carter (Peter), Mary Ledger (Jack) and Isla Lydford (Betty). Besides being decorative, Miss Carter, especially, showed that she could put a song over very stylishly. Other principals were Heather Collins (a pretty Fairy Sunbeam), Edward Hallett and Cynthia Tavender (King Gander and Queen Karin), Phyllis Wilmot (Gracie) and Albert Hill (Sergeant Gregory of the Gandoliers).

'Last, but positively not least, especially having to bend his back all evening, was Kenneth Dover, as Ermyntrude, the golden and most intelligent goose.

'Villagers, demons, geese &c., were played by: Doreen Campbell, Rosaling Churchill, Clifford Dover, Dennis Dover, Betty Gay, Ann Godley, Moira Grant, Rona Hamilton, June Knight, Josie Kraus, Valerie Spilsbury, Ernest Stowell, Marjorie Turner, Judith Tregear, Margaret Webb, Audrey Welstead, Eileen Welstead.

'Rad Raymond was stage manager; Queenie Gay, wardrobe mistress; Peggy Budden, property mistress; F.J. Riches and Marion Young, make-up; Frances Hodges, business manager.'

39

NEW YEAR 1950

At one minute past midnight the Forties, those ten years of conflict and unrest, were confined to history and the *Western Gazette* described the New Year's celebrations, as 1949 welcomed 1950 and a new decade:

'Scenes reminiscent of pre-war days, including singing and dancing in the Borough a few minutes before midnight, were provided by Yeovilians celebrating the advent of the New Year.

'Led by musicians, revellers from the Liberal Hall and the Assembly Rooms converged on the Borough in immense "Conga" lines and, as midnight sounded, more than 200 people joined in singing "Old Lang Syne". Afterwards, the bells of the parish church sounded their tradition welcome to the accompaniment of strident whistles from locomotives at the railway stations.'

The celebrations were in contrast to those of the previous year when the centre of the town was almost deserted. Thousands of others, preferring the comfort of their own fireside, greeted the New Year at home.'

'Watch Night services attracted good congregations at local churches, and that at the Salvation Army Temple was attended by Mrs Eliza Smith, of 14 Mary Street, now in her 103rd year. She had travelled to and from the Temple by car. Previously, at a party at her home, Mrs Smith recited five verses of a hymn that she learnt at least 90 years ago.

'The Mayor of Yeovil (Ald. B. Dening), accompanied by the Town Clerk (Mr T. S. Jewels), aldermen, councillors and Corporation officials, attended the parish church on Sunday for the first service in the New Year. Assembling in King George Street, the procession, which included detachments of the police, fire service and ambulance units, marched to the church headed by the Municipal Band. Afterwards, the mayor and officials marched back to the Council Chamber where Ald. S.H. Vincent thanked the mayor for inviting the council to attend and the Vicar for arranging the service.'

At the Vicarage Street Methodist Church a New Year's Eve Social was organised jointly by the Methodist Youth Club and the Church Choir. On Sunday morning there was the annual covenant service dating back to the time of John Wesley, and which had been held every year since its institution. Pen Mill Methodists gathered in the schoolroom for their annual social and watch night service. Several church members organised a programme of games and refreshments provided by friends of the church, were served by the Ladies' Working Circle.

Many parents and friends of the 32 members of the St Andrew's Church Choir gathered in St Andrew's schoolrooms on Friday for the choir's annual social organised by the organist Mr. Harold Rendell who also acted as the Master of Ceremonies.

Nearly 200 members of the Golf Club and their friends attended the club's annual ball at the Manor Hotel on Friday. The event was organised by a committee of five club officials, headed by Mr John Bradford, with Mr Lance Luffman as secretary, and among those present were three radio favourites well known to listeners to the West Country Saturday evening radio programme 'At the Luscombes'. They were John Bradford (who played Ted), Lewis Gedge ('Dad' Luscombe) and Michael Watson (Sid). Michael Watson also led the dance orchestra.

The Yeovil Golf Club welcomed in 1950 at their annual ball in the Manor Hotel.

The town's primary schools returned for the new 1950 spring term on 5 January but some children in the Westfield and Larkhill areas enjoyed an extended Christmas holiday. These lucky youngsters not only had a longer holiday but they were also going back to a brand new school. The *Western Gazette* reported that:

'When the children file into their new classrooms at Westfield County Infants School – the first of four post-war schools for Yeovil – on Wednesday, workmen will still be hard at work constructing the remainder of the building. The school's four classrooms and two large general purpose rooms, together with cloakroom and sanitary accommodation, were given building priority in order to relieve the heavy pressure on existing accommodation in the town particularly at Huish County Infants School. The second phase of the project – construction of the assembly hall, kitchen, head teacher's, staff and medical inspection rooms – is now in progress. It is expected that the school, which is capable of accommodating 200 children between five and seven years, will be finally completed in the spring. "Besides relieving the overcrowding at Huish, this new school will make possible the closure of two 'outposts' at St Francis Hall, Larkhill Road and the Westfield Baptist Church Hall which have been utilised as temporary classrooms for some time past." Mr A. R. McMillan (divisional education officer) told a reporter.'

The *Gazette* went on to describe the new school as being:

'Set in spacious grounds, which will be grass sown and laid out in gardens, it is the first post war constructed in the area of the South East Somerset (Yeovil) Divisional Executive, under the County Education Committee's urgent operational programme. The Headmistress of the new school is Miss E. O. Rogers, who pending its completion, was appointed to a similar post at Huish Infants' School. She will be assisted by Mrs E. Miles, Mrs U.G.E. Carey, Mrs M.A.O. Howles and Miss M.A. Ingham, all former members of the staff of Huish Infants' School.

'The County authority has accepted tenders for the erection of three further schools in the borough, namely Westfield Junior School, Milford Infants' School and Milford Junior School. Work on all three is expected to start almost immediately.'

The completion of the first post-war school in Yeovil could be seen as one of the signs of the prosperity and the good times which the beginning of the new decade promised.

40
AND FINALLY – SEASIDES IN FOCUS

Porlock Weir on a warm summer's day in 2018.

The Minehead open air seawater swimming pool was opened in 1936 and demolished in 1991.

Blue Anchor Beach in the 1950s.

Watchet Harbour and Esplanade.

BURNHAM – ON – SEA

The delights of Burnham-on-Sea.

The Marine Lake at Weston-super-Mare was opened in 1927 so that visitors could swim when the tide was out.

The small pool at the Clevedon Marine Lake in 2016. The tidal lake was opened in 1929 and renovated in 2015.

SOURCES AND ACKNOWLEDGEMENTS

Great appreciation and thanks are due to the Editor of the *Western Gazette* for permission to use articles from the *Gazette* in the book.

All the newspapers quoted in the text and the private papers of Jack W. Sweet in chapters 11 and 28 were consulted in the research and preparation of this publication.

All the images used in this publication are from the author's private collection.

Every effort has been made to contact the copyright holders but please contact the publishers if you are aware of any omissions, which will be rectified in any future edition.